The Lie of Spiritual Evolution

The Lie of Spiritual Evolution

RICHARD GOEBEL

*100% of all proceeds from the sale of this book
go to support missionaries around the world*

All Scripture quotations unless otherwise marked are taken from the King James Version of the Holy Bible.

ISBN: 978-1-58930-225-9
Library of Congress Control Number: 2008909000

Contents

Preface

When my sons were very little, they had a caricature done of themselves by an artist at a fair. They liked it because it looked just like them. Their body was dressed in some safari hunter garb or some other thing. But what made it funny was that their head was so huge on top of the little bodies. All the parts of them, and whatever they were supposed to be doing, were present in the picture; but it was cute and funny due to the distortions and improper size proportions in their bodies. I thought the artist did a wonderful job.

I have always known that to preach about Jesus is a very serious business. When a preacher stands to preach, he must know that he is dealing with, and is answerable to, eternity for what the people hear. One must not preach, or create a picture, of Christ that is not a true picture of Him. One must not preach a caricature of God. There is nothing cute or funny about making one part of God's character bigger or more defined than it really is. We live in a world where Jesus' mercy is preached so much that we think it out weighs his judgment- that's a caricature of God, it's a lie. Others preach a God that is looking for ways to put people in hell fire; this too is a caricature of the true God. Like most things in Gods creation, a true picture of God is a well balanced one; with each characteristic truly and rightly developed. I pray that what is written here would never cause grief to those who struggle to love and serve the Lord Christ. I also would not want to answer to God for making anyone feel comfortable in sin and worldly living. I pray that this will be a blessing and an encouragement to my brothers and sisters in Christ.

The Lord first laid on my heart to preach some of this message in Nottingham, England in November of 2004. I preached a series at that time and watched as God blessed His people. Since that time, I began to see just how far reaching this message was. And I thought that the opportunity to preach it again would come soon. However the Lord never had me preach it again.

More than two years later, God prompted me to put it into written form. I must confess that for quite a few months I kept putting it off. I didn't see any great urgency to write. Later, as some surprising things began to unfold around me, I could see that I should have started writing much sooner. I came under conviction as God made it very clear that my procrastination was disobedience, and that the Lord was not pleased with my laziness.

What follows is humbly offered that it may be a help to those who read it. Most of the thoughts are very simple and straight forward. I have, however, found that some of the most powerful things in the scriptures are simple, but often un-applied to our daily lives. Knowing this, I have prayed that an anointing would rest upon these words that would allow the simplicity of these thoughts to be a strength to those who read it, and not a weakness.

My only desire is that those who read this would consider the truth of God's Word, and see Him more than ever as a loving Father. He ever desires to bring a remnant bride closer to himself, that they would be a mature people who would see their sole purpose in life as to glorify Jesus. However, I write just like I talk, (and I don't talk that good either) so please excuse the manuscript and look beyond such things and see what God would say unto you.

Lastly, in a religious world filled with preachers who think that everything they have to say should be received and praised by all; I know that truth, although meant for all, is not for everyone and will not be received by all. The carnal mind cannot receive the things of God, because they are foolishness to him.

Bro. Richard Goebel

CHAPTER ONE

The Great Lie

Many people who call themselves followers of Christ have allowed themselves to accept the lie of natural evolution. People all over the world who say that they believe the scriptures to be the Word of God, will tell you that they also believe that life on this planet evolved from single cell amebas into all the complex life forms that we have on earth today. Of course, they continue, that this transformation took place over millions and billions of years. This contradicts what God say's in His word, but somehow the so called "science" is just too great to ignore- so they ignore the Scriptures instead! (I submit to you that anyone who doesn't have a motive of deleting God, and His morality, from their lives can't possibly believe in this "science", if they really take the time to study the teaching of evolution. However, in this study, we will simply look at what the Scripture teaches.) As we have come to believe the lie of natural evolution, we have also come to believe the great lie of spiritual evolution. We have come to believe that a sinner can grow into a Christian. We now accept that one type of creature can grow and morph into another type of creature. Much of so called Christianity today teaches a Man centered gospel (not the true Christ centered Gospel) that allows mankind to focus on what he wants out of life instead of focusing on allowing God to live, as He commands, through man for God's Glory. This humanistic, or man centered Gospel is preached in many ways and under many false names and methods. In the first two chapters of this study we will show how the gospel of humanism is taught and how the great lie of Spiritual evolution is being falsely sold as the Gospel of Christ.

The first truth that we must be convinced of is that we can and must <u>grow *in* the life of God</u>, but you <u>cannot *grow into* the life of God</u> – <u>you must be born into that new life.</u>

You cannot grow a sinner into a Christian, any more than you can grow a raspberry bush into an oak tree. A raspberry bush cannot become an oak tree because <u>they are two different plants, two distinct natures</u>. The natures are expressed differently and to think that you can grow one into the other is foolishness. And when we see what the scriptures teach about man and his state before God, it is just as foolish to think that an unsaved man can "grow into" a Christian; they have two completely different natures, they are two different beings, two distinct kinds of beings. Let's take a look at some foundational truths from God's Word and see if we can understand what I mean by these statements.

The Book of Genesis is the "Book of Beginnings"

Creation declares the Glory of God. (The heavens declare the glory of God; and the firmament sheweth His handiwork. Ps. 19:1) God said "let there be" and there was. No evolution, the Word was spoken and the Word accomplished that which it was sent to do. (*For as the rain cometh down, and the snow from heaven, and returneth not thither, but watereth the earth, and maketh it bring forth and bud, that it may give seed to the sower, and bread to the eater: so shall my word be that goeth forth out of my mouth: it shall not return unto me void, but it shall accomplish that which I please, and it shall prosper in the thing whereto I sent it. Is. 55:10-11)*

The creation of mankind, Satan's rebellion, fallen angels as demon spirits, the very existence of evil and the entire evil spiritual realm all have their beginnings in Genesis. Man's fall and man's nature being changed begins in Genesis. Fallen man is rejected by God. After sin enters in, man's nature is not good, it is evil. It is not of God but of the devil.

It is these foundational truths that the Book of Beginnings lays down in the first few chapters. <u>These are foundational truths</u>, on which all other truths must stand. If you deny, disallow, or explain away any of these things-you cannot end up anywhere but in error. This is why the Devil and his ministers try so hard to discount these truths. If he can make these stories allegorical, or we can be made to view them as poetry, or diminish their truth in any way, then we can never end up in truth. The true Church cannot be moved away from these foundation truths. If we are moved away from these things then we miss many other critical truths on which the entire life of God is built.

The Law of the Seed

For this study, the second thing we must establish is the law of the seed. Simply stated, an apple seed can only produce an apple tree. It will never produce an orange tree. If your dog is going to have babies, you can be sure that the little guys that are going to be born will not be giraffes. And when a penguin's egg hatches, you will never get anything but a penguin out of that egg. Why? Because from the very beginning God established that all things will bring forth after its own kind. Scientists can speak of evolutionary theories all they want. But when two cows are bred together, they can't show one time where anything other than a cow was produced. You may get different colored calves; one may be very large and another maybe the runt of the litter, they may have different "personalities". But after they are born, any 4 year old child will still be able to tell you that it's a baby cow. They'll never call it an alligator, a dog or anything else, no matter how different it looks from its parents. Yes, I know it's simple, but this law is one that most Christian churches have ignored in their teaching today.

In Gen. 1: 11-12, God declared that the grass, herb and fruit bearing trees would "bring forth after its kind, whose seed is in itself." In Gen 1: 20-21, God said that the creature in the sky above and the creatures in the seas would "bring forth after his kind." And in Gen 1:26-27 God "created man in his own image, in the image of God created he them" ("them" means man and woman, male and female of the human race). In every one of these instances, "the kind" that is being referred to is a nature or a characteristic. If a bird has baby chicks, not every one of the babies will be a carbon copy of the parents. There may be variations in color, temperament, size, etc. God is a God of variety, and will show us his glory in many different ways in nature. But every one of those baby birds will have the nature of a bird. They will be born knowing how to receive food from the parent. They will either know how or will have the ability to learn how to fly. They will chirp like a bird. Not one of them will roar like a lion. They will have the nature of a bird, "after their kind" because the parents will "bring forth a seed after its kind".

When man was created in the IMAGE OF GOD, What image was that? The Bible says that "God is a Spirit and they that worship him must worship him in spirit and in truth." (Jn. 4:24). The image He is talking about was the nature and characteristic of God himself. This is a Spiritual image. Obviously, if He created Adam (a male) and Eve (a female) both in his image, it is ridiculous to think that the image spoken of has something to do with the *physical* appearance. The very fact that a man and a woman are made in the same image, clearly shows us that it's not a physical thing. A man and a woman don't look alike. The image we are dealing with is a nature, a character, a seed after his own kind that is of the same nature!

Man was created a spiritual being, governed by the Holy Spirit of God. Mankind was living in communion with God and in fellowship with God. His eyes and heart were spiritually governed, thus they were naked but not ashamed. They were spiritual beings and not carnal, thus God could fellowship with them without any hindrance. So long as mankind lived with God according to His authority, man lived in a paradise, in eternity without death. Man knew no fear, no shame, and no unrighteousness. How could he? They were living in accordance with the image that they were created after, the nature of God. Mankind was the image of God and after His kind.

When Man sinned against God, the very nature of man changed! He was no longer in the image of God because man had chosen to allow sin to enter in. There was now a change. Mankind looked the same outwardly. Adam and Eve didn't get taller or shorter. They didn't get fat or thin. They still had two eyes; they still had hands and feet. The change was one of the nature.

They now had a different kind of nature. Mankind was now governed by a natural, carnal mind. Death & sin became part of his world, and a Holy God could not have any fellowship with that kind of a being. The nature of man was permanently defiled!

The Truth of Man's Sinful Nature

The first and greatest truth that has been lost in much of today's church world is that of the fall of mankind. When mankind sinned against God, there was a change in the nature of that creation that is no longer taught in much of today's preaching. When sin entered in, man became a totally different kind of creature than the one that God had created in the beginning.

Man was created in the image of God. He fellowshipped with God, man enjoyed communion with God, man was literally linked with God by the Spirit of God. It was the mind of God that enabled Adam to give names to the animals. Man was as pure as God was pure, thus they lived in the paradise of God's presence, and did so with no need for clothes. They had no hunger, no disease, and no hindrance to being in God's presence. They lived in eternity, with God, outside of time. They lived with no experience with evil or understanding of disobedience. They lived in the presence of God because man was created in the image of God. Living in the presence of God is what *that kind* of creation does – <u>it was in its nature to do so</u>.

When man sinned against God, he became a totally different kind of being. He didn't just make a mistake. The nature of mankind changed from being in the image of God to being in the image of Satan himself. Where there was once fellowship with God, there now would be strife with God's Spirit. As soon as sin entered in, man's first experience was one of shame- which was not part of the original nature. As soon as sin entered in, man began to look for ways to cover up his nakedness. Because he was now the type of being that was against God in his nature, man even covered himself in a way that God was not pleased with. They covered their nakedness (sin) with fig leaves. When God covered their nakedness (sin) He immediately covered them with animal's skins. Thus, God had shed the blood of an innocent animal to use its skin to cover man's nakedness- a shadow of the sacrifice of The Lamb of God that was to come.

When God came looking for Adam in the garden, man experienced a fear of God that had never been there before. Fear, like shame, had not been in that garden before, because fear and shame were not in God's nature and therefore were not in man's nature until sin entered in.

Why all these differences? Because man had become a different kind of being. There was a total break with the old nature, and a total break with what God had created. When God put man out of the garden, he put an angel with a flaming sword at the entrance <u>so man couldn't get back in.</u> That sword turned every which way! The reason that it turned every way was because <u>that nature would not enter into God's presence under any circumstance. No matter how that fallen nature tried to enter back into God's presence, God was saying NOT SO! THAT KIND OF CREATURE WILL NEVER COME INTO MY HOLY PRESENCE! No religion, no studying, no philosophy of life, no ceremonies, no spiritualism, no mysticism and no humanism will get that fallen nature by that flaming sword that God put there to keep us (our evil nature) out of his presence.</u>

Mankind had become a totally, and completely different kind of creature in the fall and God was stating everywhere and for all time, "that kind will not enter into my presence."

It is this understanding of the fall that we have missed in today's preaching. Man was created in the image (nature) of God, but now we live in the image (nature) of Satan. The nature of goodness was changed into the nature of evil. Where there was once light, now darkness prevails. Where there was once fellowship with God in the cool of the evening, there is now total rejection by God's Spirit. Where there was life is now death and bitterness has been substituted for sweetness. The incorruptible has now become perfectly corrupt. The spiritual has now become carnal. The friend of God has now become the enemy of God. The nature of the creation has become something all together different, to its core, and God said "I will not have that kind of nature dwell in my presence".

That kind of nature *had always been barred from God's presence,* but now mankind had become *part of that which was already rejected by God*. God is Holy and no sin can come into His presence! The fact that sin cannot be in His presence, was determined by God's nature before mankind fell into sin.

You, dear reader, may say, "That is so simple." I agree! But it is this simple truth that has been greatly lost in so called "Christianity" today. The loss of this simple truth has caused many to miss out with God, because they never knew how to get to God; specifically because this simple truth was not preached to them from the beginning. How else do you explain the utterly false teaching that has been propagated as the Gospel in today's "church"? We spend hours telling each other how great we are. How much God loves us. How much God wants us to prosper. We convince ourselves that we are on the path to becoming like God, because we go to church or because we don't rob banks or kill people. We learn how to speak "seed faith" and bring ourselves into such a state of greatness that we are to "become like gods." I'm told that one of the biggest preachers on television today now teaches that "God saw something good in you- that is why He saved you." What a lie. What a total misrepresentation of what the Bible teaches, but thousands come to here this man preach each week. Yet we won't ever deal with the awful, sinful, carnal, "enemy of God" nature that we are. We tell people to come to "the altar" because God loves them and wants to be their friend. We go through all types of emotional gymnastics to get folks to come to the altar, "because God needs us, because our life would be sweeter with Jesus in it and because Jesus desperately loves us."

Not so, God hates us (our nature) (Ps. 101:3-8, Ps. 119:104, Prov.6:16-19). Not so, He is angry with the wicked every day (Ps. 7:11). Of course He loves us, He came to earth and died a cursed death to buy us back from hell, and make a way for us to spend eternity in heaven with Him. But to take that truth, and make it a lie by telling people that God loves their sin and their nature as they are, is heresy. Furthermore, to tell them all they have to do is pray a little prayer asking Jesus to be their personal savior; and then they can go their way- and live as they want to live and God will accept them into heaven; IS THE WORST KIND OF A LIE!

If you really want to know what God thinks of our sin, look at the Cross that he endured to take it away. Our sin is so awful that he allowed himself to be stripped, beaten and crucified on our behalf. *But that wasn't the worst thing he suffered for us.* The worst thing he suffered was that he allowed himself to be attacked by all of hell, by all of sin and darkness as he hung on that tree for us. (There is a song that says "He knew me, yet He loved me. When He was on the cross, I was on His mind") He became sin for us, and the awful price of that sin was laid upon him. Thus, the cry of "My God my God, why hast thou forsaken me?" Forgiveness is not free; it was purchased at a very high price. A terrible price because God, in saving us, was going to allow mankind back into his presence, yet still be a Holy God.

The physical beatings, the back laid open to the bone by Roman whips, the thorns in his head, the 3 pound steel spikes driven through his hands and feet were the least of the pain he suffered. The greatest sacrifice Jesus made was suffering our wages of sin; and becoming sin for us (2 Cor. 5:21). He opened himself up to all that Satan and his demons could do to him as they gnashed upon him with there teeth. The spiritual warfare that he allowed himself to endure was much greater than the physical suffering!

Why? Why would he suffer such things? Yes, because he loves us. Because he wants us to have fellowship with Him here, and live with Him in eternity. But why did he have to suffer such awful things at the hands of His own creation (mankind, Satan and all the demons of hell)? I'll tell you. The redemption of man was so costly, because the fall of man was so drastic. Mankind had become a totally different kind of creature. His nature had become _evil_ and only the pure & sinless blood of God, could buy us back from that state. Only the blood of God could wash away our sin and cause such a change in us, that our very nature could be turned back to God. Only the cleansing blood of God would be effacious enough to wash away that corrupt nature and reach into our corrupted, evil, hateful hearts and change our nature back into (as it was in the garden) the nature of God himself. Jesus had to pay the wages of our sin. Those wages will be paid for every sin, for every evil thought, for every unkind word. The wages are death and the wrath of God. That is why Jesus came and died, and rose again. To take the payment for us, to set us free, and that our very nature could become a nature that God could fellowship with again. Forgiveness is not free; it was purchased at a very high price! If we really understood the awful cost of our forgiveness we wouldn't take sin and worldliness so lightly in the church! If we really considered the price that was paid for our freedom from sin, we wouldn't be as careless as we are with "forgiving" such awful worldliness   in those that drag the name of Christ through the mud in the church; only to do the same thing again tomorrow! Forgiveness is given by God to those who REPENT! And turn from their wicked ways!

This foundational truth of mankind's evil nature and the need for redemption through repentance, is one truth that is greatly ignored by most preaching in today's so called Christianity. This is why our churches are filled with sinful, nasty, selfish people who do not have the nature of Christ. The truth of repentance isn't preached because we have come to believe that we really aren't all that bad. True repentance (which is the turning away from that awful sin nature and crying out to God because we are filthy in our sins and hopeless to help ourselves) is what we've missed. Our churches are filled with people who don't even know that this is the Gospel of Jesus Christ. How can that be? Because they came forward in some altar call somewhere and some preacher lied to them and told them that all they had to do was ask Jesus into their life and they would be saved. That's a lie. Our churches are filled with people who were told that they needed to add Jesus to their lives to be happy and fulfilled. That's a lie. They have been told it would be good to come to church and pay tithes. That's a lie. Our congregations are filled with people who prayed a little prayer and were told that if they said they were sorry for disappointing God in their lifestyle he would forgive them and that He would give them eternal life. That's a lie. And of course most were told that they needed to join some church and become part of some denomination in order to serve God. That is a lie!

Each of these things that the preacher told them may be a small part of the truth, but unless that old sinful nature is exposed and dealt with, it all falls short of what God intended. Man must see himself for what he is- a total rebel towards God. When he sees that there is a Holy God, and that there is no hope of reaching that Holy God because of his wickedness, then we know that God is really dealing with man's heart. That is where true repentance begins; and without true repentance there is no salvation – no forgiveness. God, give us preachers again that will cry to a sin sick world to "repent or perish." (Luke 13:3, Matt. 3:2)

The truth is that we hate God, because that is our nature. We are the enemy of God because that is our nature. We have no hope of heaven because heaven is not in our nature- hell is in our nature. There is no good thing dwelling in us. We are totally against God, we are in revolt against him (and His nature), and He is angry with us every day. We stand under the judgment of God, and have nothing to look forward to except the fiery indignation of God's wrath. And when the time comes, He will tread out the winepress of his wrath Himself. (Rev 14:19-20) He is so against the wickedness of our sinful nature that He alone will tread out the winepress of his wrath. He will not send angels or ministers to do it- but He, Himself will do it because of the offense we (our nature) have put in his face just by being ourselves (our corrupt nature).

In true salvation, the change in us must be so total and absolute that our nature (our heart, our spirit, our very core of who we are) must be changed completely. The change that God demands is literally a change from the nature of pure evil- of Satan; to the nature of pure goodness, of God. Does that sound radical to you? It is radical! It is so radical that the only way that God could describe it was by saying that it is a totally new life. So new, in fact, that he called it being "born again." He said "you must be born again" or you cannot even begin to enter into the life of God. It is so radical, that the scripture says in 2 Corinthians 5:17 if any man be in Christ, he is a new creature: old things are passed away; behold, all things are become new." Radical, right? That's right. And the more radical it seems to you as you read this- the better you are understanding it. Because the more you think about this change and what it really is, the more radical it gets. (As I write this, I have been saved and serving God for about 23 years, and it just gets more and more radical all the time, as I consider all that God's salvation really entails.) That new life in God means that your nature (the old nature) has to die and that you have to now live another life- *but we will deal more with this truth later in this study.*

It is this truth of the fallen nature of man that has to be restored to the true Church if we are ever going *to grow in* God and stop the foolishness of thinking that we can *grow into God. To really understand this, we must now look at the "gospel of humanism & the gospel spiritual evolution", define it, see how deceptive it is in light of the scripture and ask God to show us any influence that this kind of teaching may have on our life.*

CHAPTER TWO

The Gospel of Humanism

Religion Tries to Force on God, That Which He Has Already Rejected

In the fall, man became a new kind of creature, and God drove him from His presence (Gen 3:24). That kind of creature cannot and will not serve God, nor can it dwell in God's holy presence. The problem with the humanism that passes for the "gospel" today is that it totally ignores these truths. The humanists in our pulpits teach us how wonderful we are. They tell us that God will accept you as you are and take any service that you may want to give Him. Again, we will define this much further as we go along, but for now though, any thing that changes the scripture or allows man to make himself central in any way- is humanism. It is making man god instead of Christ being God.

Let's look at just some of the humanism that has crept in and now passes for the gospel of Jesus Christ. Humanism teaches that man is central. We are taught that all you need to do is add Jesus to your life. Preachers tell us to add Jesus to our lives and we will be happy- what scripture do they point to for that? The humanists teach that the life of God is "destiny to be wealthy, prosperous and at ease" in this life here on earth.

Paul got Jesus, and he was beaten, stoned, shipwrecked and finally killed. All of the Apostles got Jesus and all but John were martyred. Jeremiah was thrown into a pit after he met God. Isaiah saw the throne of God and was sawn in two. The great men of God were the off scouring of the earth that lived in caves and the world was not worthy of them!(Heb.11) (What excuse will we give, when we have wasted our lives being "happy, prosperous and empowered in our destiny" while half the world has yet to hear the name of Jesus; and we then have to stand next to these men before God?)

We seem to spend a lot of time telling each other about how much we do for God. The Bible warns us not to think more highly of ourselves than we ought. The awful thing is, that after we spend time telling each other how great we are in God, we don't have enough spiritual power to heal a headache; and we have nothing to tell the people except that God wants them to give $100 so God can give them $1,000 in return. What utter childishness! The scripture calls them Pillow prophets and carnal men with corrupt hearts. These humanistic preachers are men with no weight to them at all. They are so light, that they are blown about like a feather with every wind of doctrine.

This morning (as I write this) I watched a preacher tell his TV audience how great this other man is. He went on for 5 minutes introducing this other "great man of God" and how great it was to have him on his program. The funny thing was that the first man, the host, is a so called Pentecostal preacher who believes in the Baptism of the Holy Ghost (or so he says) with the evidence of speaking with other tongues, and has spent years teaching on the "gifts of the Holy Ghost." His guest, however, is a Baptist type preacher, who doesn't even believe that the Holy Ghost is for today. He obviously doesn't teach on the "gifts" if he doesn't believe that the giver of the gifts is present with us today! <u>While he tells you how great this other man is he doesn't care enough about your soul to consider that they don't even believe the same Gospel! No matter, as long as we can make our flesh feel good! No matter, as long as it brings in the money. Yes, and the Pharisees and Sadducees didn't believe the same things either, but they put their differences aside in order to crucify Christ, didn't they?</u>

We think too highly of ourselves! We can't even come to grips with who we really are before God. That "in me dwelleth no good thing," and that without Christ we have no hope. Where are those who understand when the scripture says "what doth the Lord require of thee, but to do justly, and to love mercy, and to walk humbly with thy God. (Mic. 6:8) The gospel of humanism teaches us that we are basically good, just a little misguided. The man centered gospel teaches us that we just need to confess that Jesus is our personal savior and then heaven is ours- no matter how we live. The gospel of humanism teaches people how to live comfortably on earth, to enjoy life, to have our best life now and to join a user friendly church. It's all about us feeling good about us, so we pet the flesh and make it feel comfortable in the church and allow every kind of worldliness in the church.

Because we have accepted the gospel of humanism, we now think we can serve God in our own strength. We have come to believe that the change from the sin life to the God life is just a short step away. "After all", we say, "we're not so far from God. We're pretty good people. God would probably like to have us in His kingdom." Haven't you seen preachers begging people to come to Jesus, as if God needs them? Haven't you seen the Hollywood stars and the rock stars of this world sitting on the stages of so called Christian TV, as the host or preacher just fawns all over them and act like God is just so lucky to have these folks in His Kingdom? What utter nonsense! What fools we are to even think that God will accept such folks on a Sunday and then bless them on Monday as they continue to make their filthy movies, their pornographic music videos and take the name of the lord in vain in every show they star in; all because we haven't preached man's sinfulness before a Righteous God. No, we have preached that we're not all that bad; we can just grow into, or evolve, into that new kind of better person- a Christian. That's a lie straight from hell, and it has taken many souls back where it came from! The scripture teaches that living the life of God isn't hard, IT'S IMPOSSIBLE! (Romans 8: 5-8, 1 Cor. 2:14) Meaning that *in me, my strength, in my old carnal nature*, I CANNOT SERVE GOD- it's IMPOSSIBLE! But if I die, and allow God to live in me, then He Himself can live the life of God through me. That is the ONLY way! We are talking about spanning the greatest chasm known to man. We're talking about changing the very nature of man. Spiritual evolution has been sold to the church as the Gospel, and for the most part we've swallowed it without even considering the poison that we've accepted. The worst part of all this, is that even though God has rejected that carnal, self willed spirit, religion still tries to force that nature on God. God says "no flesh shall glory in my sight." (1 Cor. 1:29) But what do we do? We march the flesh right into places called churches and we tell God, "You will accept this flesh." We tell God, that the fleshly, sinful, carnal nature will be accepted by him, just so long as it can sing really well. The evil nature will be forced upon Him, in His own house, especially if it can play the kind of music that gets the house jumping, or that gives large donations. You see, that awful, nasty sinful nature doesn't care what God thinks about it, it will force itself on God; or so it thinks- (be not deceived, God is not mocked) and now we are here in the age of Laodicea, and we tell God that we are what we are (which is luke warm) and that he will have accept it. (Rev 3:14 &15) So what if God wants cold or hot? Too bad!

Some have settled for being religious. Not hating God-seemingly, but not radical disciples either- no, just luke warm! We tell God we are rich and we are increased with goods. We have so completely studied and taught the scriptures that we now have become gods- in fact we have need of nothing! (Rev 3:17) We can now tell God what we "command" him to do by our speaking the right word of "faith" We can sow "seed faith" and God has to honor it because after all – we are the Kings kids!

What utter deception! Many of the biggest names in religion today preach this nonsense every Sunday, and the huge crowds just eat it up. Never mind that they can't produce anything that even resembles the Book of Acts. God says that these men, are dumb dogs, knowing nothing; false prophets, deceivers (Is 56:10). The people tell the preachers not to preach truth, not to tell them anything that will convict them; in fact they tell them to prophesy smooth things to them (Is. 30:10). I asked for years, "How could people accept these lies?" Then I found where the scriptures goes on to say that the people love to have it this way, so they can continue in their sin. (Jer. 5:31)

Almighty God tells that carnal nature that I REJECTED YOU IN THE GARDEN, AND I HAVE NOT CHANGED MY MIND! He tells that fallen nature, that you don't even know that you are wretched, and miserable and poor and blind and naked! (Rev 3:17) Oh brethren, if there was ever one scripture that sums up the days in which we live- this is it!

And yet we still think that we are going to force that old nature (which He has already said must die) on Him and push it in His face. How sad and pitiful we are before the Master to think our opinion even counts. *(What is man, that thou art mindful of him? and the son of man, that thou visitest him? Ps 8:4)* The scripture makes it very clear that God has totally rejected that fallen nature, and that it cannot know nor serve God.

> "For what man knoweth the things of man, save the spirit of man which is in him? Even so the things of God knoweth no man, but the Spirit of God. Now we have received, not the spirit of the world, but the spirit which is of God; that we might know the things that are freely given to us of God. Which things also we speak, not in the words which man's wisdom teacheth, but which the Holy Ghost teacheth; comparing spiritual things with spiritual. But the natural man receiveth not the things of the Spirit of God: for they are foolishness unto him: neither can he know them, because they are spiritually discerned. But he that is spiritual judgeth all things, yet he himself is judged of no man. For who hath known the mind of the Lord, that he may instruct Him? But we have the mind of Christ."
> (1 Cor. 2:11-16)

In verse 11, God states very clearly that the spirit of man CANNOT know the Spirit of God. Only God's spirit can know God. That leaves you and me and our old sinful nature on the outside looking in, doesn't it? But then He brings in the hope in Vs 12, by saying that we have not (in salvation) received the spirit of the world but the spirit which is of God. And He gave us this Spirit so that we might know the things that are freely given to us of God! And when we receive these things, we can't even speak of them using that carnal, evil nature of the old man by which the world teaches, but they must be taught with the wisdom with which God gives. Then He states the simple fact that "the natural (carnal, fleshly, sinful, ungodly) man does not receive the things of the spirit of God." In fact he goes on to say that they are foolishness to him, neither can he know them. Why? Because, he continues, they are spiritually discerned. And the carnal man cannot comprehend anything of the Spirit. The carnal man is the enemy of God, and God has rejected that nature!

God shows us his plan concerning how He will deal with fallen man, and shows us what he thinks of that fallen carnal nature.

> "Because the foolishness of God is wiser than men: and the weakness of God is stronger than men. For ye see your calling, brethren, that not many wise men after the flesh, not many mighty, not many noble, are called: But God hath chosen the foolish things of the world to confound the wise; and God hath chosen the weak things of the world to confound the mighty; And base things of the world, and things which are despised, hath God chosen, yea, and things which

are not, to bring to naught things that are: That no flesh should glory in His presence. But of Him are ye in Christ Jesus, who is made unto us wisdom, and righteousness, and sanctification, and redemption: That, according as it is written, He that glorieth, let him glory in the Lord"
1 Cor. 1:25-29

God chooses to use things and people that the anti-God nature of man considers to be weak or foolish. In using those weak and foolish things, God Himself shows us that what man thinks is *important* is *unimportant* with God. Why do we need to know this? Because it shows us that our thinking, our view and our very nature is contrary to and completely against God. By dealing with us in this way, God allows no room for that fallen nature to act like it has any place before His thrown. In Vs 29, He states the end of all this- "that no flesh should glory in His presence." He then makes it clear that Christ Himself is made unto the new man "wisdom, righteousness and sanctification, and redemption." The new man must know this because in order to be born again, that soul must come to the place of seeing his sinful nature as hopeless before God. Finally, He states again that if we are to glory in anything, it can only be the cross, by which our old man was crucified, and we have hope again in God's fellowship. Read and reread these scriptures, then prayerfully consider what God must think of "the flesh on parade" that we call "church" in this generation.

"Let the wicked forsake his way, and the unrighteous man his thoughts: and let him return unto the Lord, and he will have mercy upon him; and to our God, for he will abundantly pardon. For my thoughts are not your thoughts, neither

are your ways my ways, saith the Lord. For as
the heavens are higher than the earth, so are my
ways higher than your ways, and my thoughts
than your thoughts."

Is. 55: 7- 9

God speaks to mankind and says, "My ways are not your
ways, and my thoughts are not your thoughts. In fact, as
far as the heavens are above the earth… that's how far my
ways and thoughts are above yours!"

Other than to convict us of sin, the first work of the Holy
Ghost is to show us Jesus and to make us know that He is
different than we are. He must show us that we have no hope
of being with Him and that we have no hope of pleasing Him.
He must make us see that our nature is totally rejected by Him
and that we are the enemy of God. Are you beginning to see
why this humanistic gospel is so horrible? Do you see why
teaching people that we can teach & educate ourselves *into*
the kingdom of God is so damaging? It is this lie that causes
many to be "still born" at the beginning.

Yes, I said "still born" at the beginning. Horrible language isn't it? But look at what happens and see if you can
think of a better term. People seemingly come to Jesus, go
through some religious exercise, and then they are told that
they can serve God. God may even be truly calling them
and dealing with their heart. But they come to an altar, and
religious people tell them that a little sinner's prayer will
save them, and they don't get a new nature that is able to
serve God. They don't repent and pray through. What
happens? They answered some call or tug on their heart,
but they never had the old sinful nature dealt with by the
blood of Jesus. They have been told that they can be edu-

cated into serving God, or told that coming to church will help them. But can they serve God with a sinful, unclean nature that God has rejected? No! As we have just seen, the natural man cannot receive the things of God, they are foolishness to him. God chooses the base things of the world, and His ways are not our ways, so how could we serve Him? Thus, someone that has an experience in a church somewhere may be sincere in their desire, but they came to a humanistic gospel that doesn't tell them *how* God demands they come to Him. Now they think they should be able to have a relationship with God, but the church leaves them in a hopeless situation. They have some kind of an experience, but the "church" itself is responsible for the "still birth" of that person because they don't have the LIFE of God within them. They are dead shortly after they have some kind of experience with God's spirit. They have been "still birthed" and God is going to judge the churches and preachers for the blood of these souls.

The experience they SHOULD have had with God was to teach them that you must die, and you must receive a whole new nature and character in order to serve God. The change was to be so radical, that it only makes sense to refer to it as "being born again" – it's that drastic a *change*! Instead, the humanistic gospel that tries to educate the sinner to act like he's saved is the worst kind of curse to mankind. It throws the soul of man a life raft that has nothing but leaks and it will sink every time.

I must say it again. <u>Other than to convict us of sin, the first work of the Holy Ghost is to show us Jesus and to make us know that He is different than we are. He must show us that we have no hope of being with Him and that we have no hope</u>

of pleasing Him. He must make us see that our nature is to-
tally rejected by Him and that we are the enemy of God. It is
in view of our hopelessness before God, that mankind can
cry out to God in repentance, and He will respond with
grace and with His blood. Thank God!

This lie of spiritual evolution and growing into God's
kingdom is why our "churches" are filled with tares and
not wheat. The pews are filled with people who have never
met God, have never heard God talk to them, and they
don't have any idea why they are here on this planet. Because they never have died to self, they never have been
raised up into a new life, with a new heart and a new nature. Or, just as bad, they take great pride in their "service
to God" and take hope in the fact that they don't commit
some of the sins that they see others do; and think that this
will help them in the judgment. Yet, they are ignorant that
they (their nature) have already been rejected and sentenced
to a Christ-less eternity.

It is awful to watch people go through the circus of religion, be told they have some new power or salvation with
God, then watch them get run over by the Devil. Then,
because they have never met God, never heard Him speak to
them, they have to come up with all these religious reasons
(that totally ignore the scriptures) as to why we can't live the
way Paul, John, Esther, Isaiah, Jeremiah, Hannah and Samuel
did. Thus, our churches have to invent doctrines (like the
Holy Ghost went out with the Apostles) because we can't
produce the works of the Apostles. We tell ourselves that
healing isn't for today to comfort ourselves in the fact that
we can't heal any body with our pitiful prayer meetings that
shake no buildings. Rather than seek God as to why we
cannot do what He's commanded us to do, we just change

the commandment. If we would crucify the flesh, and begin to seek God according to his Word, we'd soon see the Book of Acts come alive in our day. (In a little bit, we'll look at how God brings about this death in us)

Spiritual Evolution or a Divine Nature

Because we have ignored the truth of man's nature, we have now fallen into the death trap of accepting spiritual evolution. We have come to believe that we can, (like the Nicolaitans) *educate ourselves into* the life of God. We have believed, almost without exception that we can *grow into* the life of God. That is a lie! You can *grow in the life of God*, but you cannot *grow into the life* of God. I need to make this point crystal clear or this whole message will be lost and we will have just wasted time. I'll say it again, you can grow in the life of God (after being born into it) but you cannot grow into the life of God.

What do I mean by that? If you accept the lie that man can have access to God by turning over a new leaf, by becoming religious or that all we have to do is pray a little prayer, you will never see the kingdom of God. If you accept the lie that all you have to do is ask Jesus to come into your life, or just join some church, or give some money to a church then you have no hope, because you have not dealt with that NATURE, OUR NATURE! You have missed it all together. You have missed the fact that God hates our sin, He hates our nature; that He called us the children of disobedience, and that the wrath of God abides on us. A sinner cannot grow into God any more than a duck can grow into an elephant. This is the lie of spiritual evolution. For one to come into the life of God, he must be born into that life. He must be translated by the spirit of Almighty God from death unto life, from sin unto righteousness and from darkness into the light of his glorious Son.

Dear reader, do you see it yet? We are not talking about "growing into" God. You cannot *grow into* God. You cannot educate yourself into the life of God. This is about your nature, the core of your being. It is about becoming an all together different kind of creature. Not about something of the mind. We are talking about becoming a new creature, with an all together different kind of nature than the one we are born with. It cannot be done by learning, by persuasion or even by great preaching. It can only be done by the work of the Holy Ghost and by the blood of Jesus as God imparts his nature to us by repentance and the gift of salvation. You, without God, cannot change the nature of man any more than you can change the nature of anything else. But in the new birth, God can give us a new nature! His nature! This experience with God will make us love what we didn't love and hate what we didn't hate.

All life is defined by its nature. Science refers to it as "innate ability." No one has to teach a kitten to drink its mother's milk, it is innate- it is its nature to do that. A fish doesn't have to learn how to live in water, that's it nature. Dogs bark, birds fly, cows eat grass and produce milk and sinners sin against God- it's in the nature.

Mankind knows how to lie, cheat, steal, lust after the flesh, covet one another's goods and do contrary to the Word of God because it's in his nature to do so. Sinners sin, not because they lack an education, not because they are in need of a church board to tell them how to live, but because they have a sinful nature. It is man's nature to live in opposition to God. That is the nature mankind got when he disobeyed God in the garden and fell into this carnal, sinful thing we call life on earth.

Sinners sin because it is there nature to do so. But thanks be to God, because of his salvation, we do have hope. Only one hope, but there is hope. The only hope is that we get a new nature. And there is a wonderful thing about that new nature- it loves God. It wants to please God. It wants to do what is right. And here's the greatest thing about that new nature that God gives his children; if we allow that new nature to govern our lives (are you ready for this) we cannot sin against God! Amazing as it seems (and it is nothing short of amazing) the new nature that God gives us upon being born again, cannot sin against God because its nature is to obey God. (1 Jn. 3:9, 1 Pt. 1:16, Mat 5:48) (We will come back to this and develop this much further in a while) But for right now, we must establish the scriptural truth that it is our very nature that must be changed if we are to be saved and that without a new spiritual nature, we have no hope of God.

Look at what Peter says about that new nature:

> "Grace and peace be multiplied unto you through the knowledge of God and Jesus our Lord, According as his divine power hath given unto us all things that pertain unto life and godliness through the knowledge of him that hath called us to glory and virtue: Whereby are given unto us great and precious promises: that by these ye might be partakers of the divine nature, having escaped the corruption that is in the world through lust."
>
> 2 Pt. 2:2-5

Look at what he is saying here. Grace and peace comes to us only in knowing God and the Lord Jesus. Some people know about God, know about the scriptures, know about religion, but that won't produce a grace or a peace in their lives. Only knowing God for themselves and having a relationship with God as the Lord of their lives will bring such blessings. He then shows us that it is according to God's divine power that we have been given ALL things that pertain to life and godliness. If man's nature is sin and death; if man's nature is ungodly and wicked, how can he now say that we have been given ALL THINGS THAT PERTAIN TO LIFE AND GODLINESS? This is impossible, unless there is a change of incredible magnitude, unless there has been a change in the nature. And not just a change, but such a change that we are given ALL THINGS that pertain to life. As we have seen, before we are born into the life of God, we are, in fact, dead in our trespasses and sins. We have no hope of Godliness for we are evil and are the enemies of God. Now he tells us that we have all things that pertain to LIFE AND GODLINESS. Do you see how drastic this change is?

If that isn't enough, he tells us that we have been called unto glory and virtue. Glory and virtue? What kind of nature does that sound like? It sounds like a new creature born of heaven to me.

Now He comes to the point of the matter. Whereby, or by these things: What things? By the divine (divine means the unique attributes of Gods very nature; of God himself) power of God himself, we have been given all things that pertain to life and godliness, and we are called to use those things to walk in glory and virtue. By these things we are given great and precious promises. What promises? To go to heaven someday? To be forgiven of our sins? Yes, but much more. We are given the promise of the restoring of the fellowship that was lost in the garden in the beginning. We have the promise of a new nature. What nature? He tells us in the next sentence. That by these promises we might be partakers of THE DIVINE NATURE. God's nature! Do you see that? We are to be an actual partaker, or to posses and live with, the DIVINE nature of God Himself.

Brethren, that is an awesome claim. That isn't talking about education. That isn't talking about turning over a new leaf. That isn't suggesting that we give religion a try, or join a church. This is speaking about a new birth. A radical change, whereby the old sinful nature is done away with and the nature of God is born within that person.

Humanistic, man centered, purveyors of spiritual evolution "preachers" know nothing of what this speaks. This lie of spiritual evolution has filled our churches with tares and not wheat. Our churches are filled with people who have never repented, never been born again and have never had an encounter with God. Thus, they have never received a new nature, and that is why our churches are filled with people who go to church on Sunday and disgrace God on Monday. Our churches spend hours preaching about faith, but we have no faith because the old carnal nature has no ability to have faith in God. We hold seminars about how to overcome fear and depression, which help not at all, because we never kill that old nature that only knows fear and depression. It's in the nature! The divine nature of God doesn't know fear or depression. God hasn't given us a spirit of fear. He gave us a spirit of His divine nature. He gave us a spirit of power and of love and of a sound mind (2 Tm. 1:7). <u>We need to be born again with a divine nature that produces divine results.</u>

Again, we can grow in God – after we have been born again with a new nature. But until we are born into the kingdom of God, we have no hope. And we certainly cannot grow or educate sinners into being Christians; any more that you can grow a tomato into a pumpkin. This idea of spiritual evolution is what accounts for almost 95% of what we falsely call the "gospel". We spend most of our time trying to teach unsaved, carnal people who have never met God nor been born again, to live in a "Christian" manner. This is ridiculous beyond the absurd. Birds fly, dogs bark, lions roar, sinners sin and Holy Ghost filled people love God and desire to live for him. It's in the nature. And you cannot change Mankind's nature except it be done by God's spirit.

The miracles in the Book of the Acts of the Apostles were not performed by men who had become educated. They were performed by a people who had met God, had their nature changed by Him and were filled with His Spirit. The total leadership of God's Spirit didn't come about in the book of Acts because they attended success seminars. The power of God didn't flow through them because they had gone to Bible school. No, they had met God, had their nature changed and had become totally different men. They had experienced a change within their spirit. They had the divine nature of God within them. They had God's life in them and could duplicate God's works, because they had His nature. (Jn. 14:12) All the while they knew that it was not themselves that was doing the works. They knew that in them, that is their flesh, dwelled no good thing. But that divine nature will do what God's nature will do and produce the same results- so that Jesus, (not themselves), would be glorified

The fact that God has totally rejected sinful man leaves us on the outside looking in. We are on the wrong side of a chasm that cannot be crossed. We are hopeless. God is angry with the wicked every day, and there remains nothing more for us except the wrath of an angry God. But praise be to the God of heaven; that is not where He left us.

God has made a way into the Holy place again. He has paid the wages for our sin, and has made a way for us to be accepted in His beloved bride. That way is Jesus himself. (Heb 10:20) By the blood of Jesus, our nature can, and must, be changed! We must die and be reborn as a new kind of creature; one that is acceptable to God. One that can have fellowship with Him, just like Adam had in the garden. Jesus has made a way back past those angels; and past those swords that turn every way against that old nature. He has made Himself the way for us to partake of the divine nature and divine fellowship.

God is Pleased With Jesus

In Mt. 3:16 & 17 the heavens opened as Jesus leaves the baptismal waters and the Spirit of God speaks and says, "This is my beloved Son in whom I am well pleased." This cannot be over emphasized. This statement is critical. God does nothing without a purpose. Every Word spoken by God has eternal and unlimited weight to it. When God spoke these words, He was making it very clear that He is pleased with Jesus! Jesus pleases God! Jesus is the man (mankind) that pleases God, and it's only Jesus that pleases God. This should be telling us that *we do not please God.* My flesh cannot please Him; and if I walk in the flesh I have no hope of pleasing Him. My only hope is to be born as the same kind of creature that Christ was and is. The only way that can happen is to be born of the same kind of seed Christ was born of.

Christ is our example in all things. As we will see later in this study, God wrapped himself in a fleshly body in order to walk among and deliver His creation. The entirety of Gods spirit could not be housed in a physical body, but all that was in the physical body was God! Jesus showed us the relationship between God and His children by how He, God's Son, walked and lived on this earth. Just as he was led by the Spirit and did always the things that pleased His Father, even so we are to walk in the same manner.

We must see how the Father leads the son. (1 Jn. 2:6) We must be born of, then lead by and obedient to the Word of God as was Jesus. He, the son, is our example of how the Father will deal with us if we allow Him to have His way.

In Luke 1:35, the Bible says that the Holy Ghost over shadowed Mary and she conceived. Mary said; Let it be done unto me as the WORD was spoken. Thus, the Word came by the Holy Ghost and overshadowed Mary to bring forth new Life that was _the express_ (an exact copy with no variations – Heb 1:3) image of God.

How about us?

> "Being born again, not of corruptible seed, but of incorruptible, by that word of God, which liveth and abideth forever. For all flesh is as grass, and all the glory of man as the flower of grass. The grass withereth, and the flower

thereof falleth away: But the word of the Lord endureth for ever. And this is the word which by the gospel is preached unto you."
1 Pt. 1:23-25

Here, we see that we are born again, not of corruptible seed, but of incorruptible seed, which is the WORD! This is the WORD that by the Gospel is preached unto us. To be acceptable to God, to be able to fellowship with Him and to be saved from our sins, the Word must come by the Holy Ghost, overshadow our heart and after killing that old nature (by true repentance and allowing the cross to do its work in us), bring forth a new life in the heart of man. A heart of light must be born where a heart of darkness once beat. This incorruptible seed brings forth after its kind, just as all seeds do. The seed of Christ (the Word) will bring forth only Christ. It will bring forth characteristics that prove it is of Christ. It is that "Seed Word" that is our hope; because that seed can change our nature from that which God has totally rejected (the carnal nature of man) to that which God is pleased with (His Son, in whom he is well pleased). God cannot be pleased with anything but Jesus, because Jesus (God manifested in the flesh- Jn. 1:14) is the only nature pleasing to God.

This is driven home when the man comes to Jesus (Lk. 18:19) and calls Him "good master." Jesus asks him the question, "Why do you call me good, there is none good but God?" Jesus was not rebuking him for calling Him good. He was good. But he was asking the man the same thing he asks us. He was saying, "You call me good- which I am; but do you actually understand what you are saying?" If the man had understood that Jesus was God, and was calling Him good with the right revelation of whom he was talking to, I believe our Lord might have responded in a different manner. But because there was no understanding, Jesus took the opportunity to teach us something. There is none good but God! You are not good, I am not good- and we never will be! However, if the Seed, or Word, is planted in my heart by the Holy Ghost, and I am born of that Word, then that seed will produce in me the life after His kind and bring forth the only life that is good- the life of Jesus. Now the battle becomes not one of trying to be good; not one of trying to serve God with a nature that He has rejected. The battle now is not trying to educate myself to the point where I will be acceptable to God. No. The battle now becomes one of simply letting that Word have His way in my life and allowing Christ to live through me. His divine nature is now planted in me, and my only struggle is to let that new nature, that new man, live the life that he was created to live. (We will deal much more with this struggle in a little bit). But for now we have to see that it is _Jesus who pleases God_, because God can only be pleased with what is good, and there is none good but God!

Christ in us, is our only hope of glory, therefore if we will glory in anything, we can only glory in the cross of Christ. For it is at the cross where God made a way for that new life to be formed in us and where we now have the hope of a changed nature from the carnal to the spiritual.

That Word of God (the Holy seed that brings forth after its kind) that is now alive in the new creature can now perform its work -or bring forth after its kind. What is the work of the Word? What kind will it bring forth? The Word that is now alive in us will convict us. It will cleanse us. That Word will purify and will sanctify us. He will make us Holy. He will lead us and guide us into all truth. (I hope you see that we could just as easily say "He" instead of "it", because the Word and Jesus are the same person – Jn 1:1) That seed or Word will conform us into image of Christ, and will deal with us *until Christ be formed in us* in maturity!

Because we are different than He is, we cannot serve Him in the flesh. Flesh must be crucified- DEAD! In that death, Christ can be planted in us, then Christ can be resurrected and live through us. That like as Christ was raised up from the dead, we also are to be dead to sin, the flesh and the devil, and raised up by His Spirit into a new life of God (Rom 6:14). This is what it means when the Scripture speaks of the "body of Christ." We are to be a vessel of God's expression. But, according to Gal 5:15 & 16, a vessel not after the flesh, but a new creature after the Spirit.

I need to say, this is the basics. This is not deep teaching. This is the A,B,C's of the Gospel. This is where we get in with God; this is the only hope we have. This is THE GOSPEL OF JESUS CHRIST, I know of none other. Yet, sadly, because we have accepted humanism and evolution and not identified them to be heresy and blasphemy, the church has now come to accept spiritual humanism and spiritual evolution as the gospel. The church has now come to fully teach that we can GROW INTO CHRISTIANS. This is the greatest error in the church today! This is why most of "Christianity" is not Christian. Most of "Christianity" today has no concept of what God expects of His people. And this explains why most preachers and pastors today wouldn't know God if he showed up in their church! They've never met Him before! They just went to Bible school and learned something, got a degree in psychology, and got a job speaking and counseling in a big building they call a church!

You cannot develop into God! We can grow in God after we are born into God, but you cannot grow or educate a man into a Christian- impossible! You must be first born into the kingdom of God by the incorruptible seed bringing forth life in you. Then, and only then, can that life of God grow you into a closer place with God.

You can't grow an apple tree into an orange tree. You can't grow tomatoes into corn, Jeremiah 13:23 says you can't change the Ethiopians skin, you can't change the leopards spots, and <u>you can't teach a man accustomed to evil to do good.</u> AND YOU CAN'T GROW A SINNER INTO A CHRISTIAN. Yet that is the "gospel" we preach today.

CHAPTER THREE

The Awful "Form of Godliness"

Ways We Try to "Grow into God"

For the most part, we have come to believe that to become a Christian is no different than becoming a mayor, a Buddhist, a doctor or any other thing in life. If we just study enough, work hard enough and get the right people to accept us as some thing; there you have it- you are that thing! You can turn over as many new leaves as you'd like, but none of these things can make you a Christian. No dear reader, a Christian is a creature that is BORN FROM HEAVEN AFTER HAVING AN EXPERIENCE WITH GOD!

Consider these commonplace things in our churches today and see if you can convince yourself that we haven't come to believe in spiritual evolution. These are just some of the ways we really show that we don't believe the scriptures; but we think we can educate ourselves into the kingdom of God. In doing so, we have come to a place where we have a form of godliness, but we deny His power.

1   Translations of the scriptures:
We translate the scriptures over and over again. Supposedly, we do this to "help us understand the scriptures." We keep telling ourselves that the reason we don't understand the scriptures is because of the translation. Wrong! The

reason we don't understand the scriptures, is because we are not born of God. Jesus said, *"He that is of God heareth God's words: ye therefore hear them not because ye are not of God."* *John 8:47.* People who are born of God have no problem understanding the Word of God. Our problem lies in thinking that we can dumb down the scriptures enough so that the unsaved mind can understand them. We've already seen that the carnal mind can never understand God (1 Cor. 2:11-16). No, our problem is that we are trying to teach the things of God to people who have a nature that God has already rejected. Churches today waste time teaching people who hate God (whose very nature is against God, who have no way of knowing God in their unsaved state) from translations of so called bibles, in order that they might improve themselves, have better relationships, feel less stress or get rich. Utter nonsense, calling this silliness the gospel!

Get a person convicted of their sin and their wickedness before a Holy God. Get that person to utterly repent of their evil ways, and get them to cry out to God for mercy and get them born of the life of God- and they will understand the scriptures just fine. Every time they read the scriptures, God almighty will talk to them so much that they won't have time to worry about the scriptures that they don't quite understand yet. God, by His spirit will speak to that new heart that is hungry to know God. And those scriptures that are not understood yet will be understood later as they grow in the life of God. Amen! THAT IS THE GOSPEL.

2   Believing "things" are the blessing of God
The unsaved heart will always covet things, thus our tare filled churches must feed that fleshly lust in order to keep the carnal people entertained and happy. It is now

common to teach that the life of God will bring you success. Big names in religion now spend every service telling their congregations (both present and on TV & Radio) that it's their destiny to be rich, to have the good things in life. An entire "mini-denomination" has now sprung up around this cult of so called blessings. They are identified by the buzz words of "dream builders", "success seminars", "fulfilling your destiny", "changing your world", "overcomers", "wealth builders," "impacting your world" and a dozen other silly slogans that let people know that *"if you come to our church- we are going to tell you how to get MONEY and THINGS and be SUCCESSFUL!"*

Since when did the riches of this life have any bearing on whether you were blessed of God or not? This idiocy mocks those holy servants and handmaidens of God that Hebrew 11 speaks of as living in caves, rejected of men, the off scouring- of whom the world was not worthy. Isaiah didn't get wealth with this world's goods- No; he got sawn in two for being faithful to his God. Jeremiah didn't get a big house when he preached, he got put in a mud filled well and left there. Paul was beaten, starved, stoned, shipwrecked and finally beheaded – I guess he never did understand the principle of "sowing seeds" in order to be blessed with things. The amazing thing about all of this is that the scriptures show us exactly what this kind of teaching is.

> "If any man teach otherwise, and consent not to wholesome words, and to the doctrine which is according to godliness: He is proud, knowing nothing, but doting about questions and strifes of words, whereof comes envy, strife, railings, evil surmisings, perverse disputings of men of corrupt minds and destitute of the truth, sup-

posing that gain is godliness: from such with-
draw -thyself. BUT GODLINESS WITH
CONTENTMENT IS GREAT GAIN. For we
brought nothing into this world, and it is certain we can carry nothing out. And having food
and raiment let us be therewith content. But they
that will be rich fall into temptation and a snare,
and into many foolish and hurtful lusts, which
drown men in destruction and perdition. For
the love of money is the root of all evil: which
while some coveted after, they have erred from
the faith, and pierced themselves through with
many sorrows. But thou man of God, flee these
things, and follow after righteousness, godliness,
faith, love, patience meekness."
1 TIM 6:3-11

The reason this type of "faith" and "success" oriented
ministries thrive is because that is what tickles the flesh of
the unregenerate heart of a sinner. Did you notice that
from this kind of teaching comes envy? What do you call
it when people want everything that others have? Did you
notice that he said which some covet? The nation of
America will be judged because of its wickedness. But the
one of the greatest judgments of God will be reserved for
"preachers" who not only thought it all right with God to
be COVETOUS, but also taught the world to be so! A man
who thinks he is "evolving" into something "great" looks
for these types of teachings.

But a man born of the incorruptible Word will follow
after true godliness. He's not interested in the toys of this
world to convince himself that he's blessed of God- thinking gain is godliness. No my friend, to the man born of
heaven- godliness is the great gain he is looking for.

3   Faith Ministries

We waste hours of preaching on faith because our congregations are filled with the faithless. Does anybody ever wonder why the big names of religion can preach pretty much the same message week after week, and yet the people don't have any real faith? Of course the people don't have faith in God- they have never met him. Of course they don't have faith; faith is the nature of God, not fallen mankind. Our churches are filled with people who think their struggle is to have faith. Wrong! My struggle is not to have faith, my struggle is to do away with the old nature and let Christ be formed in me. When Christ lives in me as he desires, faith is a natural character of that new life. The reason we have to *teach* faith is because it's not in the nature of the congregation to *have* faith. The super star preachers spend every service (when they are not trying to get your money) trying to teach faith. You can't teach a fish to bark like a dog, it's not in its nature! And you don't have to teach a fish to swim- it's in his nature. You can't teach the unsaved to have faith in God, and you don't have to teach the born again to have faith in Christ- it's his nature to do so. I know after we are born into God, we have to grow in faith, but those who think that's what these so called preachers are doing are blind.

This is just another way we try to "grow into God", instead of coming to God on his terms, and being born a new creature that has a faith within because it has Christ living within the heart.

4   We teach carnal doctrines that we can "touch and feel"

Any time you teach salvation or the life of God based on a doctrine that man can handle and control, you have a gospel of humanism. True believers are perfectly confident with the true salvation of God that cannot be seen and controlled by man, because once they meet God- that is the only kind that can quench the thirst of that heart for God. But the sinner who has never met God will desperately need to touch, taste, control and handle the things of salvation. The carnal nature will have nothing else because he knows of nothing better.

There are so many things that go on in our churches today that have nothing to do with God. But these same things are the mainstays of whole denominations and religious organizations because they help the tares "feel" like God is with them. They are the natural, man controlled, carnal things that we use in order try to convince the "un-born again" that the "anointing" is present or that because things look like God is here, everything is OK, even when it isn't.

Look at just a few areas that we have substituted the natural for the spiritual- so that man can control his salvation.

a) *Water baptism for salvation*: if you think that getting a sinner wet changes his nature from an enemy of God to a child of God, that's just sad. But whole denominations have arisen telling people that they must go down into water to be saved. You know why, because a carnal, "un-born again", unregenerate heart will not accept a salvation based on an experience of meeting the Savior. Not on your life, they want to have something they can get their hands on and say "this is it, this is my salvation, and this is why I am a child of God." Pitiful man, still trying to force that rejected nature on God.

b) *Teaching that "tongues" is the Holy Ghost:* The Holy Ghost is not poured out on the unsaved. You must be born of God to receive this Gift of God. So the carnal mind of man comes up with a way to tell him he has God's spirit. He makes tongues the Holy Ghost, then teaches himself to speak some gibberish, and then tells everybody he has the Holy Ghost. Such nonsense is not deserving of a response, but… When a man has repented of his sin, cried out to God for forgiveness and is born again, cleansed by the precious blood of the lamb, the new man inside is a fit habitation for the Spirit of Jesus to come and dwell in. When that new man cries out in faith to God for the promise of the Father, God will give him the gift of the Holy Ghost. When the Holy Ghost comes, one of the things he will do is fill the vessel to overflowing, and when that happens that most unruly part of the flesh (the tongue) will be submitted to God and God will give that tongue a heavenly language to communicate to God with. The Holy Ghost will give you tongues, but speaking in tongues doesn't necessarily mean you have the Holy Ghost of God. If you're not born of God, and you mess around with spiritual things and leave yourself open to a spirit- you may end up with a spirit but it may not be the Holy Spirit.

When I hear about folks who spend all their time teaching about tongues, instead of teaching about the Holy Ghost and why He comes; I just wonder if it ever occurred to any of them that the hundred and twenty in the upper room had never even been told that they would speak in tongues? In fact they were waiting for a "promise", and they assumed they would know when it came.

Only a carnal mind would think to get control of something like "tongues" in order to tell everyone that they have the Holy Ghost. Why? Because the old sinful nature will not stand for being told that is has to pray through to meet God, and that God Himself will fill with his Spirit and give a new language. No, that flesh wants to control that; and thus they control the "tongues" thinking that they control the Holy Ghost. Silly preachers have taught this nonsense for years to a congregation of tares who all jumped up and got excited over tongues. The real miracle of tongues isn't that I speak in an unknown tongue, the miracle is that God himself overshadows this life and brings even the most unruly member (the tongue- Jam. 1:26, Jam. 3:5-8) under subjection and He gives a language that is especially for Him and for His use and that we speak directly to God.

c) *People "run and dance in the spirit" others "fall out"* under the power: I know that these things may happen in a genuine move of the spirit of God. But when you start making these things the test by which you can tell if God is moving, you've missed God by a mile. When God is moving, people will not be waiting for "catchers" to get behind them before they "fall out". When God moves, you don't have to worry about someone falling and getting hurt. If it's really God they will be just fine, and if it's just the flesh wanting to play a game, then they ought to get hurt.

Many years ago, when I was just saved, I once watched a true servant of God go to lay hands on a man that was at least 6 foot 4 inches tall and he weighed at least 280 pounds. I watched, <u>and the preacher's hand got about 6 inches from the man</u> as he was going to lay his hands on his chest and pray for him. <u>Before the preachers hand ever touched him</u>, I saw the power of God hit that man so hard that he literally left his feet and slammed into a wall that was at least 5 or 6 feet behind where he had been standing. The collision was so violent that I remember thinking three quick thoughts. My first thought was that the man literally flew back as if he had been hit by a car. (I actually remember thinking about a car striking a body and sending it through the air upon impact because that is really what it looked like to me). My next thought was that the wall would have to be fixed because there was no way that this particular wall (it was not well built and of flimsy construction) would take such an impact and not be broken. And along with that thought, I just knew that this man was going to be so sore when he "woke up" from the power of God coming upon him like that. I spoke to him after the service and he had no idea of my concerns. He just told me that all he was aware of when God came was the warm presence of God and that he felt just wonderful in the after glow of Gods presence. I learned well, this is not a natural thing- it's spiritual. Today, the carnal mind wants to play with the things of God, so we have catchers to make sure people don't get hurt. We have people run around and cover ladies with blankets so they don't look indecent. I cannot believe that the Holy Spirit of God would ever do something to a daughter of Zion in such a way so as to leave her indecently exposed for the eyes of those about her- no way! There are countless testimonies of the wind of God blowing through a service and souls ending up under and over chairs. I've seen heads bounce like basketballs as the Spirit of God knocked people down, but I can tell you- if it's really God there won't even be a sore spot when the Spirit lifts. No my friend, all the gimmicks of religion are just the carnal flesh playing at the true things of God to make himself feel like all is well. But all is not well unless we know God, and unless He knows us. When the real Holy Ghost of God has written "icabod" (the glory of the Lord has departed) over the house and left it, all that's left is man trying to play at the things of God. How sad that we shout for joy over such foolishness. We can teach the carnal to act like God is present, we can dance and fall out, but sooner or later God will make a breach and then we'll answer to him for the games we've played.

d) *Ministers dress in special robes to look like they know God.*
   How foolish we've become. We see more and more of these pretty boys on television having "special services" where they dress in some robes or some frock to let everyone know that they know God. When Paul entered a city he came humbly and in meekness, but when he preached all men knew that he was a man touched from another world. History is filled with men who were anointed of God, who could not impress any one with their education, but no sickness stood before their prayers to God for healing. When Samuel came to a town, the people began to quake and ask weather he came to fellowship or to pronounce the judgment of God. This was because Samuel was God's servant, not because of how he dressed. However, since our Bible college educations can't produce any results of this kind, and since the devil doesn't know these men any more than he knew the sons of Sceva, our powerless preachers of today just dress like they're special, and try to

look like they have an anointing. And the carnal nature of man does what? It says "oooh and ahhh". It says "doesn't he look Holy." The prophet said "the people love to have it so." It makes no difference that the man can't produce anything of the life of God- just so long as he looks good for the flesh.

e) *Worship has to be entertaining.* It now has to be taught. When you are born again of God's spirit and you've been forgiven of all your sins, that new nature will automatically love to praise God. Today whole church auxiliaries exist just to teach people how to worship, and to spend hours practicing our songs so that our worship can be just right. How many of our big time choirs spend hours in fasting and prayer, pleading with God that the anointing would be upon their singing so that His presence in the song service would break the yokes off the lives of the congregation or visitors? Most of the so called great song leaders today don't look any different to me than the world's famous entertainers. Its all about them, saying "look at me- I'm so talented." They're not interested in God getting all the glory- it's a show of the flesh. I want to make it clear that I am not saying there is anything wrong with a church choir practicing so that a song services can be had. But when it becomes an elaborate show, that entertains the flesh, <u>it has become an evil thing</u>. When the choir sings, so that the congregation can just sit back and enjoy the show, then it has become something that is unscriptural. Since when was it OK for me to go to God's house, sit back and watch a show. The scripture teaches that it is required of me that I worship God with all of my heart. (John 4:23-24) True worship is when I pour out my soul before God in praise and worship that flows from my heart. As a matter of fact, that is the only kind of worship God will even accept from me.

Jesus said that God seeks after a people who will worship Him in Spirit and in truth. In Spirit (not in Flesh-SPIRIT) means that it must come from within me, from the depth of my being – not some rehearsed thing that the flesh had to practice until it sounded good to the human ear. In truth (not in false spirituality-TRUTH) means that I worship Him, because I know Him and love Him, and the worship is in truth because it flows out of a real relationship with Him. When people are really born again of God's spirit, the praise and worship is simple, done in faith, and is not a learned exercise. True worship is something that comes from within, out of the inner most being before the presence of a Holy God. We have come to a point now, where "praise" to God is entertainment- not a Holy offering to the Lord.

Do you know one sure way (there are many) how I can prove that most of the worship in our churches is totally of the flesh? It's simple enough to do. Tell the congregation that there is going to be a "worship service" at the church and tell them some big name music artist is going to be there and only give them 2 days notice about the "worship service". And make it on a week night, so that they have to get up and go to work early the next morning. Get the picture? What will happen? Your congregation will be there, they'll invite friends, and you'll have visitors from other congregations. You'll have a full house! Now, at the end of that "worship service" make an announcement that there will be an all night prayer meeting coming up from midnight to 6am. Give them a month to prepare and to schedule it into their busy lives. And make it on a Friday night so that they can go home and rest on Saturday morning. Tell them the only person who is going to be there to lead the prayer meeting will be Jesus. Tell them there will be no music, no food, no talking; just time to spend on their knees praying to the Lord for his will to be done in His people. What will happen? How many of that big crowd that came to "worship Jesus" at that "worship" service will be there? You know the answer. If you go, you'll have your choice of seats to pray at. Why? Because the flesh isn't entertained by prayer. No, you won't get 10% of the tare filled congregations we call houses of God in today's godless religion to come out for a real all night prayer meeting! We've made it all a parade of flesh that man controls to make himself feel good.

Does that sting a little? But is it true? I pray that what you've just read doesn't seem harsh or critical. But if we're going to be honest with ourselves; we know it's the truth.

f) *The inability to produce the life of God.* The whole emphasis of religion today is to make products of a religious system- not disciples! If you look at all the work done in churches today, what does it really produce? It creates people dedicated to some religious idea or to a system. Jesus is not real in their lives. They are not committed to Jesus. This is because we have come to think that we can study and educate ourselves into a system or pour others into a mold; and we then act like that religious system will lead us into God. Utterly false. Religion without the life changing experience with God always leads to death.

g) *We assemble in large numbers.* This is totally defiant of all scripture! Show me any where in the Word of God, where God dealt with the masses. No, it was always a remnant that was serious with God that He spoke to. We gather the goats together by the droves, and then we act like God has to honor us because we are strong in number. Carnal. We gather in numbers because the flesh likes to feel like it can hide in a big crowd. The carnal mind that has never met God can only judge by what he sees with the carnal eye. That is why we take such great comfort in large numbers. We hope that "this many people can't be wrong. God must be here." Of course, we forget that only Joshua & Caleb entered into the Promised Land. We forget that only eight souls were in the ark. Jesus, after dealing with the religious minded people of his day; was left with only 12, and he asked if they would leave Him too. Remember, there were only 120 in the upper room after all of the miracles were done! The carnal mind, untouched by heaven, can ignore all these scriptures (and dozens of other examples) and take comfort in large numbers!

h) *We have substituted a gospel of humanism for the Gospel of Christ.* Because we have the unsaved in the church, that never met God, <u>we then try to grow others into God with a SOCIAL GOSPEL</u>. (Because that is all we have to offer- if we can't offer a Living Christ or demonstrate His life and Power)

1 We give food to the hungry, but never warn them of the fires of Hell

2 We build hospitals for the sick, but have no power to lay hands on the sick so that they would recover.

3 We build mental institutions because we can't cast the devil out of the possessed.

4 Our preachers study psychology because they can't discern anything by the Spirit of God.

5 We have all kinds of fund raising events to spread the gospel, only to produce religious images of a system- not Christ like people.

6 We give to the poor, but never tell them of their spiritual poverty and the impending judgment against their bankrupt soul.

What do these kinds of ministries produce? I know that the Bible tells us to help people and give to others. I know that Christian people will minister to others in need, as the scripture teaches. But when we make that <u>natural help equal to the Gospel we have totally missed the point.</u> Look around the world today and you will see hospital's that bear religious names on the door, "mission" ministries that give to the poor, and myriads of other ministries that have so called Christian names and do good works. My only question is- where is the life of God being produced in all of these places and ministries.

Shortly after being saved, my first encounter with a "Christian Mission" was a place that had been around for almost a hundred years and provided a place for homeless people to sleep and bathe. There was also a store that sold used furniture and household goods. The proceeds from the store went to help the poor. I'm sure that when someone started this mission or ministry, they probably were

Christian, and they probably saw the ministry of helping the poor as a way to share the Gospel. A hundred years later, as I walked through the place there no evidence that it was even supposed to be a Christian place other than the name on the door. The people working there were not Christian. There was no mention of God or Jesus. It was simply a place where drug addicts and homeless came to eat and sleep.

This is not unusual; in fact it is most common. Most people have no idea of who William Booth was; they have no idea of what the Salvation Army was when he began the ministry. Can you imagine the employees of a Salvation Army store gathering today for what Mr. Booth called "knee drills" and pray and cry out to God for souls to be saved with fasting and prayer? Hardly! We now have come to think that these kinds of so called ministries are doing "Christian" work. Why? Because this is the kind of social gospel that we now preach in the pulpit and the average person on the street can't tell the difference. Most people have now come to think that this is the Christian gospel.

A book which deeply impacted my life is "Revolution in World Missions" by K. P. Yohannan, a man who has spent almost his entire life on the mission fields in areas of north India where there are 500 thousand villages that have never even heard the name of Jesus; not even once. These people are the poorest of the poor who live in very hard and primitive environments. (If not the whole book, I wish every American Christian could read chapter 4 of this book. I still try to read at least this chapter every few months to try and keep the impact fresh on my life.) Yohannan makes the point very strongly about the damage that a social gospel has done. He then writes that he has spent his life preaching the gospel to those who have never known what it is to have enough to eat. He has seen the poorest of the poor come to Christ and have had their hearts and nature completely changed. <u>But he has never shared the Gospel of Jesus with anyone, seen them come to Jesus and be truly saved and converted - and then had them respond with a request to be given food, clothing or any such thing.</u> These souls rejoice to know that God loves them and that He has forgiven their sins. They are free. They are delivered! Their joy in salvation causes them, in most cases, to go and tell others about this Jesus. He has seen people who have gone to preach, yet they themselves have nothing to eat and only the clothes on their backs. The salvation of one's soul has nothing to do whatsoever with having enough to eat or a place to live. Nothing! It's only in a sin sick understanding of the Gospel that we think that there is any connection between the two! I know that to many, this is very controversial. Our religious minds are so warped that we equate "Christian ministry" with things, with meeting peoples natural needs in this life. The prosperity preachers have completely linked the blessing of God with things and wealth.

Now, I must make this point very clear. I do know that a born again believer will have a desire to show compassion to others. I know that the scripture teaches in James 2:13-22 that we have not only a duty to take care of our brother in need, but in fact our faith is made perfect in these works. I know that Jesus taught us that as often as we minister to those in need, we do it unto Him. But true service to others is an outgrowth of knowing God and wanting others to know Him too. True ministry has the goal of leading others into an experience with God, not to feed their belly or give them clothes. To make that the whole Gospel is sad!

To link Christ and His gift of salvation to the goods of this world, is the mindset of a cursed people. To even suggest that _food, clothes or things_ have _anything_ to do with ministering Christ's salvation to a lost world just shows how ignorant we have become. A lost soul needs Christ. Not food, Christ. Not clothes, not doctors, not things, not help-CHRIST. Only Christ! Do you know how many people are fed in soup kitchens, sleep in shelters and are treated in medical clinics all in the name of Christ? Yet these same people who receive this care are never told that Jesus died for them or that he hates there sin and that they can be free. Are they ever told that the devil can be cast out and that they can be free of the addiction that binds them? When Jesus ministered to the poor, he told them to sin no more. He told them that they were to live for God and He set them free of the things that bound their lives in chains. Again, I'm not discounting that a saved heart will desire to look on the needs of brothers and sisters, but that is not a substitute for preaching Christ. Haven't we yet learned that if people come for anything other than Christ then they will ultimately destroy that church? If they come because they will get food but they won't repent of their sin, what good has it done them? If someone attends a church just so they can receive some natural care, and they die and go to hell in their sins; and we have not warned them of the judgment of God, we will be held accountable for their blood (Ez.3:17-27). If they come for the music or friendships or even for good preaching, they will be lost anyway; and they will become a stumbling block to those in the church around them. When will we learn this?

What has been the result of this kind of "ministering" without preaching Christ? Over the years I have dealt with many people who have come to our church right off the streets of Philadelphia, for some kind of help. Do we try to help them? Of course we do. But when you see them come for food or ask for money; as you try to help them, if you try to tell them about Jesus, many times they very boldly tell you that they "didn't come to hear about that stuff. They came for food or money." I've had them tell me *that I have to give* them money because I am a Christian. I've had them tell me very angrily that they don't want to hear about sin, about heaven or hell. They just want money and if I don't give it to them they curse me and leave; and tell me I'm not a Christian on their way out the door. I had one man tell me loudly and with much venom in his voice, that we were not a real Christian church if we didn't give him any food. He also told me that he didn't want to hear about his drugs, his fornication and his sinful life before a Holy God! A Muslim woman told me that she just wanted money, but wouldn't come in to the church service because it would make her impure to worship a false God. I told her that my God could deliver her from her life of drugs and sin, she left upset that I wouldn't give her money.

I wouldn't mind when these things happen, but what bothers me is, <u>who taught them that this is what the church was for?</u> The humanistic preachers of the man centered gospel taught them that the church was here to give them food and money, but that the church should mind its own business when it comes to shinning a light on their sin<u>! It's the church's fault! We will face God one day and give an account for teaching such things.</u>

The church has come to think that if we can attract people by offering help to meet their needs, we can then lead them to Christ. Is that what Jesus did? Did Jesus heal people, then tell every one what he had just done, so they would serve Him? No! He told those he healed to tell no one, but give thanks to God and sin no more. Did Jesus get excited when thousands came to Him after feeding them with a free lunch? No, in fact, He told them that their coming was worthless BECAUSE THEY HAD COME TO HIM BECAUSE THEY EATEN OF THE LOAVES AND FISHES! An evil generation seeks after a sign. (Mt 16:4)

<u>We have done the opposite of what the Master did, and that is why we have produced the opposite of what He produced. He produced LIFE</u>! He produced a small group that would gladly die rather than to fail Him. <u>We produce carnal people, who love big crowds that would give anything to please themselves and to enjoy "the good life"</u>- and call it "the blessings of God."

There are so many more things that go on in our churches today that have nothing to do with God. But these are some of the things that religious organizations do because they help the tares "feel" like God is with them. They are the natural, man controlled, carnal things that we use to try to convince the "un-born again" that the "anointing" is present; that because things look like God is here, everything is OK, even when it isn't.

Any doctrine, any effort, any teaching, or anything else that man controls and makes flesh feel like all is well; is not of God and never will be blessed by the King.

What are the Results of this Evolutionary and Humanistic Gospel?

> "This know also, that in the last days perilous times shall come. For men shall be lovers of their own selves, covetous, boasters, proud, blasphemers, disobedient to parents, unthankful, unholy, Without natural affection, trucebreakers, false accusers, incontinent, fierce, despisers of those that are good, Traitors, heady, highminded, lovers of pleasures more than lovers of God; Having a form of Godliness, but denying the power thereof: from such turn away. For of this sort are they which creep into houses, and lead captive silly woman laden with sins, led away with divers lusts, Ever learning, and never able to come to the knowledge of the truth."
>
> 2 TIM. 3:1-7

Look at how clearly this scripture speaks to our day. He establishes that the times in which we live will be perilous! The next sentence begins with the word "for" which means because. So it will be perilous because of the character traits he then lists next. He starts out with men who are lovers of their own selves because they have not come to recognize who and what they really are. They have never come to the realization that they are evil in nature, so they do what all flesh does- loves self. If we ever get a real understanding of what our fallen nature is before a Holy God, we will not love ourselves; we will love the God of mercy who paid the awful wages for our sins and saved us!

This leads to a list of character traits that describe our generation perfectly. Because we have taught this humanistic gospel of spiritual evolution, we have developed this

list of characteristics so perfectly that to not see this as fulfilled in our generation would take an almost indescribable
ignorance. Do we not see the covetousness and the boast-
ing against God? Can we not see the pride on display, the
blasphemy of our day? Our children are disobedient to
parents. We are an unthankful and unholy generation,
without natural affection, trucebreakers and despisers of
those that are good. We certainly are heady and highminded.
And we are the epitome of those who are lovers of plea-
sures more than lovers of God. Perilous times!

Then in verses 5 & 7 he gets to the end of the matter;
the results. Because we have preached spiritual evolution
and because we have made the Gospel a social gospel of
works and natural helps, we are now left with a people that
have a form of godliness but deny the power thereof.
Doesn't that sound exactly like our day?

We have a form of godliness. We have built huge build-
ings, gathered in large numbers, have many Bibles, dress
the part of church goers, talk of what great things God wants
us to be- but in every thing – WE DENY THE POWER OF
THE GOSPEL. If we really believed that a burning lake of
fire awaited every soul that died without Christ, would we
spend all of our time building schools and clothes centers
for the lost? If we really believed that God was the healer –
would we spend hundreds of millions of dollars building
hospitals and putting some "Christian" name over the door?
If we believed that a missionary was doing a work worth
supporting, could we drive fancy new cars and have a big
screened TV's in our homes, and yet not be bothered to
support a missionary and his family for $40 a month? If
we believed that others were perishing without Christ, could

we spend money on newer and more comfortable chairs for the congregation (when the four year old ones are just fine) rather than doing without so that the work of God could be supported; so others might know Jesus? We have a form of godliness, but in reality we totally deny the power of the gospel.

So where does that lead us? <u>It leads us directly to verse 7 of 2 Tim. 3, where God shows the miserable end of our evolutionary gospel. He tells us that we are "ever learning and never able to come to the knowledge of the truth."</u>

You see, sometimes the hell we get isn't even the hell God intended. Sometimes the judgment is our own creation! Since we now teach that educating a people can save them, and that teaching the sinner to act like he's a Christian makes him righteous before God, we now have that as our reward. We learn and teach; and teach and learn. Then we teach and learn and learn and teach. We have seminars and books and tapes and CD's and DVD's. We have conventions that draw thousands. And we learn more and teach more; and teach more and learn more. AND WE NEVER COME TO THE KNOWLEDGE OF THE TRUTH! Christ is truth, and we have set Him and His Gospel aside. So we learn and learn and learn on the treadmill of religion. On that treadmill, we never move anywhere, we never enter into rest, we just become tired and worn out. And we don't even realize that we have doomed ourselves to the awful sentence of ever learning, but we are not able to come to the knowledge of Christ. Oh, that we might know Christ!

Notice that He used the words "never able" to come to the knowledge of the truth. He didn't say that we would miss it; he didn't say that we would choose this end; He didn't say that we would be on the path and just come short. No, He said that we would be "never able". Why would he say "never able"? It is because, as we have already laid out in this study, we have set aside the basic principles of the Gospel. We are completely unable to access Christ. Our very nature is unable to comprehend Him. We have denied God's *rejection* of our evil nature. We have refused to come to Him in repentance, forsaking all, as He has demanded. And now we are on the religious treadmill of ever learning. Don't you see it? Look at the world of "Christianity" today. Don't you see a people, who have a form of godliness, deny the power of God and who are ever learning? But in the end, we are unable to come to the knowledge of Christ. God deliver us from ourselves.

In conclusion of this part of our study, we must understand that we are carnal and have no hope of entering into God's presence, much less pleasing Him. Our nature is evil and has been rejected by God. But, because we now think we can evolve into being children of God; we have produced a church filled with people who have no desire or ability to serve God.

If we are ever going to have a hope of pleasing God, we must have our very nature changed, we must be saved! We must meet God and be born again of the Spirit and the Word of God. We must understand that the seed or Word of God will conform us to the image of Christ because when the incorruptible seed is born in us, it will bring forth after His kind. The Word, conceived in us, will bring about a change in our nature from one of darkness to one of light. And it is this new nature that, when it prays, God will hear, that God can talk to, that God will be pleased with because it is the nature of Jesus. It is this new man, not the old that can please God.

Now if we understand this study to this point, we must now deal with the next truth in this study. The new nature is a Spiritual creature born from above; yet there is still an old nature (because we are human, living on this earth) and the old, carnal man must not only be crucified but he must be kept crucified. We must now understand how the new nature needs to rule over the old nature so that it can serve God as it is its nature to do. We must also recognize the reality of the old nature and how God will help us keep it crucified. We must also learn how and why there is a war within us as we struggle to grow in God after we are born again. Lastly, we must come to recognize the roll and purpose of trials in our life after we come into the life of Christ.

CHAPTER FOUR

Growth in the Life of God

The Old Man and the New Man

We must now look at the great conflict within the new believer. The new creature is now born again within the new believer. The "new man" has a desire to serve God, and God will hear when that new man calls on His name. This new creature is born in the image of God. It is born after the image of the seed (Word) that brought him forth. Therefore it is Spiritual, Godly, and Holy. It is a nature that desires to serve and please God. If all of this is true, the next great question that must be dealt with is; why then is there a struggle to serve God within a newly born again believer?

We must be honest and deal with the following questions. "Why do I still have ungodly desires if I'm really saved?" "Where does this fight come from if I really love God?" "Why does the born again believer still have a war within himself to trust and obey God?"

Not only is it fair for the believer to ask these questions, but if we don't seek after an answer to these things, we are going to end up in a religious mess. I believe that it is right here where most of so called "Christianity" has veered into a spiritual ditch! We must face these questions and answer them in a way that strengthens our relationship with God. And that will only happen if we answer them according to the Word of God. We cannot and must not come up with our own doctrines and thoughts as to how to answer these very real and honest and critical questions. It is absolutely crucial that the new believer come to an understanding of what goes on within the heart and spirit of every new believer. I believe many, many new converts get saved, have an experience with God and then spend years in turmoil because no one ever teaches them the things that we will now look into.

The word of God shows us two specific things that we must now look at. Firstly, when the new creature is born within a person's spirit, there is still present an old nature that must be crucified and kept crucified in order for that new man to serve God. Secondly, there is a work of sanctification that must be done within the new believer. I want to say again that we cannot "grow <u>into</u> God", but this part of our study is vital, because we will never "grow <u>in</u> God" if this area is not understood.

> "This I say then, Walk in the Spirit, and ye shall not fulfill the lusts of the flesh. For the flesh lusteth against the Spirit, and the Spirit against the flesh: and these are contrary the one to the other: so that ye cannot do the things that ye would. But if ye be led of the Spirit, ye are not under the law."
> GAL. 5:16-:18

The commandment given tells us to walk in the Spirit, because if we do we will not fulfill the flesh's (the old man's) desire to sin against God. The next sentence states clearly for us, so that we don't think we can serve God with the old man, that the flesh and spirit fight and lust against each

76

other. The flesh will keep us from doing what we would do. What would we do? After that knew birth, the new man would serve God and please him because it is the nature of Jesus which always pleases God. And the only way that this can happen is to be led of the Spirit of God, and in doing such we have been delivered from the law. What law? The law of sin and death. (We will deal with this much further in a minute, but for now we have to establish that there is a battle between the old man and the new man.)

> "And the very God of peace sanctify you wholly:
> and I pray God your whole spirit and soul and
> body be preserved blameless unto the coming
> of our Lord Jesus Christ."
> 1 THES. 5:23

Here, God shows us that we are made up of spirit, soul and body. It is the spirit that has been changed in the new birth. The soul is our mind and our thinking. When we are saved and born again, our soul which is the mind realm is still present. We have the same memories, the same habits and the same thought process that we had before meeting God. And of course our body is still the same. The key to this battle between the old man and the new man is *to understand who* is in the battle and *to know how to insure the victory God has provided.* (This part of our study could easily take many pages and be its own bible study, but for this study we must see that the new man is the spirit man, created after God's image in the new birth. The mind, or the soul, still has the power to make decisions.) When we come into Christ, that new nature can serve and please God, but the mind and body only know the way of the old sin life. We now must go through the process of learning how to allow that new nature to rule over the mind and body which have always ruled in the old life. He prays that God would sanctify us wholly. Wholly, here means that our spirit, our soul and our body would come under the blood of Jesus. Sanctify means that the new man in us would come to rulership over our minds and our bodies. (Rom 12:1 & 2). It is this growth process, or sanctification process that we need to consider now.

The Process of Growing in God

One of the greatest preachers of the last hundred years, B.H. Clendennen, has made two statements that I wish to quote as we start this part of our study. The first statement is that "re-generation is sanctification begun, and sanctification is re-generation continued." The second statement was "that if we preach sanctification as anything other than a person (Jesus) we will split the church." (1 Cor. 1:31) These two statements are, in themselves, so vast that if the church could just get a hold of these truths, much of what the church argues over would be left behind as we go on unto perfection is Christ (Heb 6).

When something or some person is sanctified unto God, it means that it is set apart for God's use. And being set apart for Gods use, it is never again to be returned to secular or worldly use. A person that is sanctified is to be a vessel that is completely cleaned and surrendered and ready to serve God and to carry out His will. This certainly is contrary to what we have just learned about the old sinful nature of mankind. The new creature, however, is sanctified (after his kind) because it is born of the incorruptible seed. But the new creature must grow up and take on its full characteristics. This will happen unless something stunts its growth. The new creature will mature and take on all the attributes of the seed from which it was born (after His kind), just like a puppy will grow into a dog, an acorn will become an oak tree, and just like a new born child will grow into a full grown adult.

When it's born, a child has all of the genetic code that it will ever have; its mind functions and body parts are all present, but that doesn't mean that it is mature. That new born baby has legs but can't walk, has a tongue but doesn't speak words etc. These are things that must be learned, but it can learn them because it is in its nature to do so.

The new creature, born again by the Word and Spirit of God is just like that new born baby. That new creature must grow into maturity and learn to function as a mature person. But for that new man to grow into full maturity, we are going to have to understand that there will be a battle. The battle will be between that old fleshly mind and body that can't serve God and cannot receive spiritual things; and the new man who is born of the seed of God after His kind. There are two fountains present; one of sweet water and one of bitter water. There is a nature that desires God but there is yet present a nature (that old soul/mind realm with all its habits and ways) that desires the world. And if we are going to ever mature in the things of God, we will have to understand this battle. Look at the battle that rages within a man of God like Paul:

> "For we know that the law is spiritual: but I am carnal, sold under sin. For that which I do I allow not: for what I would, that do I not; but what I hate that do I. If then I do that which I would not, I consent unto the law that it is good. Now then it is no more I that do it but sin that dwelleth in me. For I know that in me (that is,

in my flesh) dwelleth no good thing: for to will is present with me; but how to perform that which is good I find not. For the good that I would I do not: but the evil which I would not, that I do. Now if I do that I would not, it is no more I that do it, but sin that dwelleth in me. I find then a law, that, when I would do good, evil is present with me. For I delight in the law of God after the inward man: But I see another law in my members, warring against the law of my mind, and bringing me into captivity to the law of sin which is in my members. Oh wretched man that I am! Who shall deliver me from the body of this death? I thank God through Jesus Christ our Lord. So then with the mind I myself serve the law of God; but with the flesh the law of sin. There is therefore now no condemnation to them which are in Christ Jesus, who walk not after the flesh but after the Spirit. For the law of the Spirit of life in Christ Jesus hath made me free from the law of sin and death."

ROMANS 7:14- 8:1

Here, Paul is describing the war within himself. He hasn't lost his mind and he isn't confused. But as we read it carefully, we can see the war raging, why it goes on and the victory that God provides. He starts by stating what we have already been establishing in this study: that the law of God is spiritual but our old nature is carnal. He then describes the war of wanting to obey God, but finding that the flesh wants to fight and disobey God. The things he wants to do (in his heart that desires to do what is right) he doesn't do (because the flesh fights to sin). And the things that he doesn't want to do (in his heart that desires to do what is right) he does do (because the flesh fights to sin).

Remember the commandment to walk not after the flesh but after the spirit. Because if we be led of the Spirit, we will be free from this law of sin and flesh.

This leads to the recognition that the new man really is born of God because for the first time, there is a genuine desire to please God and a great sorrow of heart when we fail Him. Thus, he can say that it is no longer he (the new man) that fails God, but sin (the old nature that has NOW BEEN REJECTED BY, NOT ONLY GOD, BUT BY PAUL HIMSELF). This is not an excuse or a license to sin; just the opposite. This is recognition of the change that has taken place by the great mercy of God, as well as by acknowledging our own wickedness before the God of heaven. He describes the attack of the sinful nature upon the spiritual nature that delights in obeying God.

With this recognition comes the cry of "oh wretched man that I am, who shall deliver me?" A question that always comes to the true believer who struggles to please God! He then praises God, because God alone can and did deliver his soul. Then he concludes the whole point of the matter by stating once and for all that it is his desire, his intent and his choice to be faithful to God. He recognizes, however, that the old man (the flesh) will never desire to or be able to serve God; but it will always serve sin.

Lastly, he teaches us a critical lesson in being victorious in this battle. He states unequivocally, that because it is the old nature that sins against God, we are to focus on and develop the new man and not allow the devil to beat us up every time we fail God. He says that when God shows us our sin and our failures, we are not to be under condemnation as long as we are IN CHRIST. God does not show us our failures to condemn us; He shows us where we are so that we can grow in Him and learn more of His ways. He does this as a loving Father corrects his children so that they can grow up to be better servants for His purposes. The key is that he says there is no condemnation to them that are IN CHRIST, WHO WALK NOT AFTER THE FLESH BUT AFTER THE SPIRIT! I've heard silly preachers use this as an excuse for sin or to teach that God will accept them sinning against him. They missed the whole point. If we willfully sin, or we choose to ignore God's Word, then we are no longer IN CHRIST, we are now outside of Christ. If we allow ourselves to be deceived by our own heart, we will come up with all kinds of reasons to think that God will accept our disobedience, but then we are no longer those who WALK NOT AFTER THE FLESH BUT AFTER THE SPIRIT. We would be walking after the flesh, right? At that point, it's not a Father chastening his children with love; but it can quickly turn into an angry God pouring out his judgment upon that rejected nature of mankind. Do you see what we are saying here? This is critical for us to understand. God is not a mean God who looks to destroy his children with guilt when they fail Him. Neither is he a doting old grandfather whose grandchildren can do anything they wish and he will just accept it. He is a Holy God whose judgments are true and righteous all together. He is a loving Father and the God of heaven. Thank God that the law of the Spirit has made us free from the law of death!

After being born again, one of the first things that a new believer must come to grips with is that there is still an old nature present. This nature is that soul, the old mind that has the habits of the old nature that was trained to disobey God. The soul and body must be brought under subjection to the spirit man which is now born of God's Word. There is an ongoing process by which the new creature must mature, must grow up and take on its characteristics. This sanctification (growing up), is the process by which God matures (conforms to the image of Christ) the new creature and empties out, does away with and crucifies the old nature. Our God does this out of love, and takes us through this process because He needs mature Christians who can represent Him and do His work. There must be a maturing (sanctification) of the new man, and a decrease and death (crucifying) of the old man. Why? Because the new creation, born of God's Word, will serve Him and bring forth fruit; but with the flesh (the old evil nature) we serve the law of sin. John the Baptist said "He (Jesus) must increase but I must decrease." We know that John was speaking of his own fame and ministry giving way to the ministry of Jesus, but spiritually we must see that process in our lives as well. We, our old nature, our old way of thinking, our feelings about things etc. must decrease until all of that is dead and crucified because it hinders that new man from serving God. And Jesus, His ways, His thoughts, His feelings and His life must increase until only Jesus is seen in us! This is what is meant when Paul writes in Galatians

> "I am crucified with Christ: nevertheless I live; yet not I, but Christ liveth in me: and the life which I now live in the flesh I live by the faith of the son of God, who loved me and gave himself for me."
>
> GAL 2:20

That is the end of this process for every believer if we allow God's full work in us.

CHAPTER FIVE

Growing Through the Trials

The Purpose of Our Trials

If we are to become *mature* Christians, we must understand that God's whole dealing with His children is to decrease us (our old nature) and to increase Himself in us. (John. 3:30) This process will begin the day we are born again and will never finish until we awake in His likeness as we stand before the Lord of Glory. How does God bring about this decrease in us? How does God bring about the growth of the new man to a place where we come into the image of Christ in maturity? As we read the scriptures and pray over them we will begin to see many characteristics that God will want us to develop. We will also see things that God will want us to drop from our lives as well.

We must allow God to teach us these things and to work them out in us if we are to enter into the fullness that God wants for His children.

As a loving father, God will teach us, work with us and bring us into maturity as we allow Him to deal with our lives. There are many ways this is done, but one of the ways God will do this is by allowing difficulties in our lives. We may think it would be nice if we could simply learn about the life of God by instruction, like book knowledge. But as we will now see, this is not really the case. Many of the greatest growth places in our lives will be in the things through which we suffer…our trials. We don't like to hear that, but what does the scripture teach us? Jesus was sinless God in the flesh, but He was our example in all things. In Hebrews 5:8 we read "yet learned he obedience by the things which he suffered." In Philippians 2:8, we read that Jesus "humbled himself and became obedient unto death."

If we are born again we must follow Jesus' example. If we are going to serve God and be of any use to Him at all, we must suffer and learn obedience; and learn to humble ourselves. We must strengthen the new man so that he now controls what the old nature has always controlled until we were born of God. That old man was always in control, now he is being crucified. If you think that the flesh just goes away quietly, and stays crucified like a nice little puppy dog in a corner, you are not a spiritual person! That old man will do everything it can to stay alive and to destroy that new creature. That is its nature to do so. Look at how careful we must be when dealing with that heart of man.

> "The heart is deceitful above all things, and des-
> perately wicked: who can know it? I the Lord
> search the heart, I try the reigns, even to give
> every man according to his ways, and according
> to the fruit of his doings."
> JEREMIAH 17: 9 & 10

If you read this carefully, you will see that God tries our wicked hearts in mercy so that the judgment can be avoided. When God deals with the new creature (remember he doesn't deal with the old nature at all, it's been rejected by God) here on this earth, He does so according to Romans 8:1 & 2. He corrects us and reproves us. But He does this out of love, and we need to understand that He only corrects us because He loves us. We are not to come into condemnation when He shows us things in our lives that displease Him. He doesn't do this for condemnation, He does it as a loving Father trying to help His children mature and become what they were created to be. And He does this now (on earth) in mercy and in love. We must keep in mind that when people who die in sin stand before God's judgment, there is no mercy to be had. Any sin, any disobedience, any thought that is displeasing to God which is not under the blood will be dealt with by God in judgment. The key here is that, while here on earth, there is mercy and forgiveness through the blood of Jesus and the mercy of Christ; in the judgment there is only the wages of sin-which is death, poured out with the wrath of God against all evil.

It is in our struggles and trials that we not only crucify the old man and build up the new man; but many times it is in these trials that we realize we are not where we think we are in God. God has a purpose in our trials; to bring about our correction and growth.

God Reveals To Us Our Hearts

In Exodus 14 & 15 we see one example of the reason for our trials. In Ex. 14:10-12, the people who have already seen the great miracles of God that brought them out of Egypt, look up and see Pharaoh approaching. Do they now think of those plagues upon Pharaoh and take great confidence in God? No, they are filled with fear and begin to murmur against God and in His servant Moses.

God then tells Moses to lift up his rod over the waters and God parts the red sea, and the people walk through on dry ground. In Verse 28, Pharaohs horses and chariots are swept away into the sea and destroyed. Now it is important to watch what happened next. The Bible tells us that the people believed and feared God. We cannot minimize the fact that the Scripture says that they now believed and feared God. They did believe God, at least to some degree, because the scriptures tell us so.

In Ex 15:1-19, the people sing a beautiful song of Worship. They sing of God's power and glory. The song of praise is so wonderful that the scripture records the whole song.

Then in verse 20 & 21, Miriam and all the women sing and dance with timbrels. At this point, if you asked these people about their faith in God, they would have told you that they trusted in God. They would have recounted to you the great things God had done for them, and they would have told you that they would trust God from now on.

And here's the key thing, they would have probably not been lying to you. They may have honestly believed that they had come to a place where they would trust God and obey him from now on. But God knows our hearts, even when we don't.

In verse 23 & 24, we read what was really in their hearts. There was no water to drink and the people began to murmur and complain again. God uses our struggles to show us where we really are. Notice, <u>they sang the right song.</u> They praised God and worshipped Him. <u>But they sang the song AFTER they went over on dry ground. They praised God AFTER they saw their enemies destroyed</u>. They thought they had grown in God to a certain place, but in the next trial we see where they really are. They are still doubting God and murmuring against His servant and complaining about the life of God. Even while they were singing the praises of God, it was this murmuring and doubting spirit that was really in their hearts. But at the time they sang their song of praise, no preacher could have convinced them that God was still displeased with their unbelief, and that they had a complaining heart that God was angry with. But in his mercy and grace, God used the next difficulty to show them the things in their heart, (that old man) so that they could repent of the unbelief and draw closer to God.

If they had sang the song of praise BEFORE they had crossed over then that would have been a testimony. More correctly, it would have been *their* testimony. They would have believed what was not yet seen. (Heb. 11:1) Do you see that although they sang a great song of praise, it wasn't really their testimony yet? No, that was Moses' testimony, because he believed God BEFORE the sea was parted. The people only thought that they had the testimony of God's greatness. <u>But in the very next trial we see they don't really have a trust in God yet. But if God never brings them into another difficulty, they will never deal with that old man that is still present</u>.

This is a picture of how God will deal with us if we are going to become mature, fruitful Christians that are sanctified and prepared for His use. If we don't get an understanding of the fact that there is a new creature born of God, but that there is also an old nature present that must be done away with; we will have one struggle after the next and never become mature enough to understand what God is trying to do in our lives. This old nature, this old mind, the old self life with its sinful habits must be overcome by the new spirit man which is being led by God. God will use struggles to show us what is really in our hearts.

God will use the struggles in our lives to strengthen the new man. In Ex 1:12 the Scripture tell us that the more God's people were "afflicted, the more they multiplied and grew". God uses these trials and struggles to help us understand that the old man will never serve God and that only the new man, that nature born after His kind, can serve Him.

This principle is critical for the believer to understand, or he will never understand the fight and struggle that goes on within their own heart in their service toward God. I've seen many people who have been saved, but they continually get beat up by the devil; they want to serve God, but like Paul, they become aware very quickly that there is still this old nature that has a habit of sinning against God. The devil beats on their mind and tells them they are not saved. The unsaved around them say "I knew you didn't change" or "I thought you were supposed to be a Christian" when they do something that is less than Christ like. This is because there is an old nature and a new nature that are now present. God will help us overcome the old man as we seek Him for grace and understanding. But our faith must lie in God's Word, and in knowing that the new man is born of God and will bring forth after its kind if we let it mature.

[I need to make something very clear at this point. Any time we study the Scriptures, and how God deals with Mankind, we must keep a proper balance in view. I want to encourage the child of God who struggles to obey God, but I am not making any excuse for sin in the lives of Christians! There is no excuse for willful disobedience. God will not tolerate lazy Christians who use His mercy and grace as a reason to live unholy and ungodly lifestyles. Worldliness and any friendship with the world makes us the enemy of God. This part of our study should make our heart hopeful, and it should make us see how much God loves us; and deals with His children as a loving Father helping a child grow up. This truth should encourage us not to give up when we fall short of God's holiness. When we fail God and He corrects us, as a loving Father corrects his children, we should not feel forsaken and feel like giving up.]

[On the other hand, we also know that we live in a world of "greasy grace", and the Un-Christian way in which many so called believers live. This part of our study is not meant to make the disobedient soul feel at ease with their sin. Nor does this condone those who have been in church for five years and still "struggle" with fornication, stealing, worldly lifestyles that bring the name of our God to shame! God judges righteous judgment and He measures the heart of a person. God deals with His children who fail Him as a merciful Master, but with the disobedient or calculating deceiver He will deal harshly. ***Be not deceived, God is not mocked, we will reap what we sow!] Gal 6:7***

In Exodus 23 God lays out this principle in such a clear way that we should be enlightened and very encouraged. In Ex. 23:20 God says He (His angel) will go before them and keep them in the way and bring them into the prepared place. He then tells the people to be very careful to be obedient, and in verse 23, God tells them that He will go before them and lead them into the battle against their enemies. Read verses 24-28 and God says over and over "I" will do this; "I" will do that. But even though the scripture says 'I", meaning God, don't we have a part in the growth, in the victory in the occupying the prepared place? The "I" is God, but it's really a "we" thing; because the Christ in me is God. And the new creature in me will have to live out its intended nature and service toward God.

The 'I' is God. God says "I will do this on your behalf. But the new creature, the new man, the Christ in me is that which God will deal with. God will lead, God will guide, God will give victory, but the "I" does not mean that we have nothing to do. When God says "I" will do it, does that mean that we will not have to fight? Does it mean that we will always be at ease and have no problems? Of course not! We are commanded, as soldiers of the cross, to pick up the sword and enter into the battle.

God Uses the Battles to Bring About Four Needful Things

1   God shows us where our hearts really are and what is in our hearts. It's when God leads us into the difficulties and into the battles that we gain some very valuable things in the life of God. The first of which we have already seen. In the midst of trials, God shows us where we really are and what is in our hearts; he shows us our faults. In the battles of life, we learn about what's in our heart. We can see if we really have come to fear and obey God, or are we

just rejoicing because we have seen another miracle- like the Israelites at the red sea. When we come short in the struggle, we must keep in mind that God shows us these places where the old man still rules (or where the new man needs to be matured) not to condemn us (Rom 8:1) but to bring us closer to Him. God uses these times to humble us, to correct us and to mature us. This whole process is so that we can be vessels that He can use for His glory.

2   We learn of God's faithfulness in times of struggle. We can *talk* of God's faithfulness. We can try to *convince others* (and ourselves) that God answers prayer and that He is our ever present help in the time of need. But the truth is, that the old man that hates God and that cannot trust in God, will always bring up doubts to the new man. The only way we genuinely *know that God is faithful* is if we find ourselves in trouble and cry out to God and then He teaches us His faithfulness by answering the prayer or leading us through to victory. The only way we know that God is a healer is when we find ourselves sick and afflicted and The Holy Spirit comes and allows us to experience His healing virtue. It is at our lowest point where we can appreciate the most, God's hand lifting us and causing us to cry out "my Lord and my God." It is in the darkest hour that His light becomes so precious to us. I'm not being poetic here; there is a reality to God's greatness, and the depth to which we understand that greatness, is directly proportional to how much we have allowed God to prove himself to us in our struggles.

"My brethren, count it all joy when ye fall into divers temptations; knowing this, that the trying of our faith worketh patience. But let patience have her perfect work that ye may be perfect and entire, wanting nothing."
JAMES 1:2-4

He tells us to count it all joy when we fall into diverse temptations. Why would he write such a thing? Because he says we ought to know that the trying of our faith worketh patience, and that we are to then let patience have her perfect work that we may be perfect and entire wanting nothing. Why would the trying of our faith work patience in us? Because if we stay with God, trust in God and don't run when the enemy comes, we will see, with our very own eyes, that God's Word is true. We will see for ourselves that Christ is really our deliverer and that He will ALWAYS BE FAITHFUL to those who will be faithful to Him.

OK, so if we really come to a place where we have proven these things, what will happen in us as we face the Devil? We will genuinely have patience in the difficulties of life because we have already come to know *that nothing is outside of God in our lives.* When you know that even the worst situations are only there to bring us closer to God, and that God ALWAYS proves himself, and provides a way of escape, there comes a sincere patience in any situation; because we know it's only temporary and that it is for God's glory.

Now, he says, "the trying of our faith worketh patience." Then, "let patience have her perfect work." Once we can have true patience in the battle, what is the perfect work he speaks of? The perfect work is that complete trusting and resting in Christ, in spite of any circumstances. So why would He then tell us that this perfect patience would make us perfect and entire wanting nothing? Because any person that is <u>totally trusting in God</u>; that is <u>completely yielded to God teaching them something</u> will be perfected in Christ. Any soul that is <u>only looking for God to be glorified</u> in any battle is a soul through whom God can show forth Himself mighty. Anyone who can genuinely say "the old man is crucified, and in this terrible situation all that matters is that I watch patiently, knowing that my God will deliver" is person with a perfect heart toward God. A servant looking only for an opportunity to glorify his God – this is the perfection that God is looking for. We must come to realize that God is not looking for anything from us except our availability to do His will and give Him glory. Thus, we will be perfect and entire, wanting nothing!

3   It is in our trials that we gain <u>our valuable testimony</u>. In Revelations 12:11 we read that the children of the Most High God overcame the accuser of the brethren by the blood of the lamb and by the word of their testimony and they loved not their lives unto death. The value of the trial for us is that we can brag on our God, that we can testify of what He has done in us and for us; not what we have heard about. Not what *He used to* do, but what we *have experienced for ourselves* of His goodness and mercy. We overcome by the *testimony that we have* after learning of God's faithfulness in the battle. If you sit back and look for God to do everything and you never enter into the fight against sin, the flesh and the devil, then how are you going to have a testimony? All we will ever have is a second hand account of what God used to do. We will always have to speak of what God has done for others, or what we heard about from someone else. But God's desire is that we know

of his goodness for ourselves; and that His life is real to us because we have experienced it for ourselves. Then, and only then, can we truly testify of God's goodness; because we know it for ourselves!

4   God will use the <u>trials in our lives to build us up</u>. It is in the fighting and the struggling to please Him that we grow in spiritual strength. It is in this growth that we can become a vessel that God can use. <u>It is in the warfare that the old man that God cannot use dies; and that the new man is built up and becomes a mighty man for the kingdom of God.</u> This is all in the process of allowing that which is born of God, (born of that seed, the Word of God, after its own kind) to express its divine nature and to mature to the place of glorifying God. That rejected, sinful nature must be crucified and the new man must be lifted up to a place of rulership.

In exodus 1:12 the scriptures says that the more God's people were afflicted the more they multiplied and grew. This principle is shown throughout the scriptures, but God's reasoning for how and why he grows us through the battles is laid out plainly for us in the twenty third chapter of Exodus.

"I will send fear before thee, and will destroy all the people to whom though shalt come, and I will make all thine enemies turn their backs unto thee. And I will send hornets before thee, which shall drive out the Hivite, the Canaanite, and the Hittite, from before thee. I will not drive them out from before thee in one year; lest the land become desolate and the beast of the field

> multiply against thee. By little and little I will
> drive them out from before thee, until thou be
> increased, and inherit the land."
> Exodus 23:27-30.

God tells us that He will go before us and give us the victory over our enemies. This is <u>a fact that God wants us to accept, that there will be victory to the obedient and the faithful</u>. In verses 27 & 28 he tells us the He will do marvelous things and give us the land. At his point it all sounds so great, everyone is jumping and shouting. But then he tells us *how* he will give us the victory; and, for some, the jumping and the shouting stops. In verse 29, he says "I will *not* drive them out before you right away. If I do that, the land (the blessing) will become desolate (it won't be fresh) and the beasts of the field will multiply against you (the devil will get in and mess it up). He shows us the growth that it will take to inherit all that God has for us. "By little and little" he will drive the enemy out. Why not all at once? Because we have to grow up, to be increased and to mature the new man so that we can occupy the land. Do you see what He is saying here? God will not drive out every problem for you immediately. You'd not know what it is to struggle. You'd never have a testimony of God's working in you. You'd never have the opportunity to see what really lies within your heart.

Also, if you have no battle, then you will never grow in strength. You will never become a battle axe in the hand of your God. God could never use you to destroy the works of the devil or to be an example to those about you. He says if I just did every thing for you, and cleared away the enemy from before you all at once, then by the time you inherited what I want to give you, it will be desolate and dry. And the beasts of the field will come in and make their home in your promised vineyard and will be multiplied against you. He wanted Israel to take over lands that had been farmed and tamed. He wanted to bring His people into a land with houses and vineyards. If the land was unoccupied for years before they got there, then it would be over run with animals. The houses would be falling down and there would be no crops growing. Seemingly, it would have been easier for God's children to just have it all cleared out for them ahead of time, but they would have missed the full blessing of the tended fields and tamed villages.

<u>To have all things easy is not the blessing God has for his children. To have great victories, to know the goodness of God and to be able to trust in Him with all our hearts – *that is what He has for us.*</u> But He tells them this will be done by little bits at a time. Why? He would do it only *as they became strong enough* and *great enough* in number to inherit the whole land. In other words, God was letting them know that as He sees that they are ready and able to advance, then He will drive out the enemy before them. This is what He desires to do for us. <u>He will give us the victory.</u> This must be a settled fact in the mind and heart of the believer. But He will give us the victory, <u>in stages as we grow to a point where we can occupy the victory that He provides.</u> That is His principle.

Militaries have known this for centuries. They know you don't take over more land than you can secure. If they find themselves in an area that they can't totally occupy and secure, then the enemy is now within their own area, and that is the most dangerous kind of battle there is. An army wants to draw as clear a battle line as possible, keep it's army together and identify all else as the enemy. Keep the enemy on one front and fight him there. An army that has to fight on the front, but also has to fight within its own area is in trouble. We must maintain the victory that Christ has provided us. Once God deals with us and teaches us about an area of our life, it is our responsibility to keep the enemy out of that area and be obedient in whatever he has convicted us about.

What good would it be for us to be given the victory in an area, only to find out the next day that the devil can just come in and destroy that area of our life and take away that blessing of God? No, <u>God will give us victories, and then He commands us to hold the ground and keep the world, the flesh and the devil out of that area of our lives</u>. We must grow into the promises of God and that can only happen as we get in the fight and do battle with the enemies of our God. This is the clear distinction between "growing in the life of God" as opposed to "growing a sinner into the life of God."

Do you think that someone who is born again and saved on Monday should be fretful about how he's going to cast out devils and raise people from the dead on Tuesday morning? What would you say to such a person when you saw them discouraged and fearful and worried about these things on Tuesday afternoon? Would you tell them that the power of God can't cast out devils or raise the dead? I certainly hope not! If that person told you that they went home after being born again and read their Bible, then showed you where they had read that they were supposed to do these things and now they were afraid of failing God because they didn't know how to do such things, what would you tell them? You would, I hope, explain to them that, "Yes these things are real and that God wants His people to come into a place of power with Him and that these things are to be done." But you would also, I hope, tell them that they have skipped a few steps. If they just got saved, the next thing to do is to receive the gift of the Father, and be baptized in the Holy Ghost. Jesus said that <u>we would receive power after that the Holy Ghost is come</u> upon us. This poor person is all worried about how to exercise the power of God and He hasn't even received the Power because He hasn't received the Holy Ghost yet according to Acts 1:8. What about water baptism as an outward declaration of what God has done in their heart according to Romans chapter 6? You would probably tell him that if they don't know any thing about what the scriptures teach yet, how are they supposed to discern that there is a devil to be cast out? Do you see what I'm trying to say here? There is a growth in God. There are things that God wants us to know about Him. And our loving Father will take the time to teach us these things if we are faithful, and follow on to know the Lord. Thus, the principle…"*By little and little I will drive them out from before thee, until thou be increased, and inherit the land.*" The whole land is to be occupied. All the fullness of the Gospel is to be lived- but not all at once.

Is this any different than a loving natural father trying to raise his child? What does a father do when his nine year old comes and tells him that they will never be able to do college math because it's too hard? What does he tell his seven year old when they are worried about how they will get a job and pay bills and raise kids? Doesn't that father ease the worries of that child by explaining to them that these are things that they will be prepared for when the time comes? He tells the nine year old that even though college math looks hard now, by the time they have 9 or 10 more years of math classes, they will be ready for college math and it won't seem so hard. He would explain to the seven year old that a child is not supposed to have the ability to get a job, pay bills and raise kids. A seven year old has a lot of growing up to do before those kinds of responsibilities are to be met.

<u>We also know that if the father removes all struggles from that child's life, and gives that child everything, that child will not be ready when those challenges of life do come.</u> If the father helps the child's fear of college level work by doing all their homework for them for the next ten years, would you consider that man a good father? If that father gives his seven year old all the money they could ever spend to alleviate the concern for a job and financial responsibility, then gives the child a soft job and a big paycheck when they are 16 years old to "help" them, would this be good for the child? No, the child will just be spoiled. That child will be unable to perform the job anyway; and won't know how to handle the money that they are given. Finally, what kind of job will such a child do when it comes time to raise their own kids? What a mess those grandchildren will be in, because their parents will be totally ill equipped to teach them anything because they themselves know nothing. Thus, *"By little and little I will drive them out from before thee, until thou be increased, and inherit the land."*

If we see the wisdom of this in the natural, can't we see God's wisdom in dealing with His children concerning the eternal? Now look at the seventh chapter of Mathew.

> "Ask, and it shall be given you; seek, and ye shall find; knock, and it shall be opened unto you: For everyone that asketh receiveth; and he that seeketh findeth; and to him that knocketh it shall be opened. Or what man is there of you, who if his son ask bread, will he give him a stone? Or if he ask a fish, will he give him a serpent? If ye then, being evil, know how to give good gifts unto your children, how much more shall your father which is in heaven give good things to them that ask him?"
>
> MATHEW 7:7-11

Jesus speaks concerning the natural father as being a type of our heavenly Father. But God is no human father who is limited by flesh, He is God almighty. God will teach us, He will lead us and guide us. And in doing so, He will see to it that we grow enough to inhabit <u>all</u> of the Promised Land that he has for us. And the enemy will be driven out before us as time and our faith allows. As we grow, He will enlarge our heart for Him and we will grow in our service for Him. This is why there are to be elders that lead a church. You don't let a novice come in and direct the teachings of the church do you? Of course not, the elders are to be seasoned, stalwart, faithful and older in the things of God. Why? It's not about physical age, but you do want elders directing, because you want people who have gone through the battles to be leading the charge, not a "green horn" that has never seen a shot fired before.

Many fellowships have been destroyed by bringing in large numbers of people just so they could say they were growing in God. However, if the new people added are not born of God, then all that was accomplished was that the flesh, the world and the devil were added to that fellowship. Then the new people come in and start to tell the church how to serve God. If the fellowship doesn't have a strong and experienced leadership that can stand for truth, then the new people added will destroy that church because they were never born of God's nature. All because the church was not mature enough to handle the "new converts." This scenario has destroyed the church as a whole. Instead of letting God add to the church daily such as should be saved we just added flesh to the sanctuary, and because we were not in a place with God to keep the victory, sin has over run the Holy Place! We must come to know this particular purpose of our trials. We must grow to become strong enough to inherit and then occupy the land.

"But with many of them God was not well pleased; for they were overthrown in the wilderness. Now these things were our examples, to the intent we should not lust after evil things, as they also lusted. Neither be ye idolaters, as were some of them; as it is written, The people sat down to eat and drink, and rose up to play. Neither let us commit fornication, as some of them committed, and fell in one day three and twenty thousand. Neither let us tempt Christ, as some of them also tempted, and were destroyed of serpents. Neither murmur ye, as some of them also murmured, and were destroyed of the destroyer. Now all these things happened unto them for ensamples: and they are written for our admonition, upon whom the ends of the world are come. Wherefore let him that thinketh he standeth take heed lest he fall. There hath no temptation taken you but such as is common to man: but God is faithful, who will not suffer you to be tempted above that ye are able; but will with the temptation also make a way to escape, that ye may be able to bear it."

1 Cor. 10:5-13.

God was not pleased with Israel for they were overthrown in the wilderness. Did you notice *it doesn't* say "God was not well pleased with them, and so God over threw them"? No, it says he was not well pleased _for, (or because)_ they were over thrown in the wilderness- or in their trial. They didn't understand the purpose for their trials, they just complained all the time. They murmured against God, they spoke against God's servant, they lusted after the world, they desired to go back to Egypt. That is why they never had Moses' testimony; and why only Joshua & Caleb testified that God could overcome the giants in the land; and why they were the only two that entered in to all the promises of God.

God says in verse 6, that these things were for our examples. Then we are commanded to neither tempt Christ in our trials, nor murmur because of the trials. They were overthrown and destroyed because of such things. Then in verse 11, God tells us again, plainly, that these things happened unto them, for examples and they were written for our admonition; upon whom the ends of the world are come. So if we think we are standing for God, we need to be very careful because of that wicked and deceiving heart of unbelief that is present in the old man. Therefore, let us know and understand, that there has no temptation taken you but such as is common to man. Why is it Common? Because all of His children are dealt with in this manner, to bring about growth; so that we can be perfect vessels for His use.

He then says God is faithful, who will not suffer you to be tempted above that which you are able to handle. Then he wants us to know that God will, along with the temptation that comes, provide a way to escape and that we may win the victory. But it's not enough for each of us to read that scripture. We must go through the trials and struggle with temptations, and see God provide that way to victory. It is in these battles, as Paul wrote about in Rom 7, that we really come to know about ourselves (the old sinful man and the new man in Christ) and the God that we serve.

That new creature will bring forth after his kind, just like the old nature will bring forth after his kind. And because that is so, God will help us purge out the old and strengthen the new that we can become vessels for His glory. That is what he meant when he said that we are to be Vessels of honor, sanctified and meet for the master's use(2 Tm. 2:21) Do you know why He used the term meet: meaning proper or prepared for? Because when a person is truly sanctified, set apart for God and has the spirit of God flowing through him, then it is only proper for that vessel to be used by God. God will always flow through that kind of Vessel. God can get glory for himself through that kind of vessel. A vessel that is sanctified belongs only to God because Christ is made unto us sanctification (1Cor 1:30) and that kind of vessel cannot be anything else but a vessel that God will use. This is the results of God strengthening the new man through the trials and tribulations of life. Thus, it is only "meet" or proper for a vessel of honor which is sanctified to be used of God, for His glory.

The Great Principle & Purpose of God's Purging

> "I am the true vine, and my Father is the husbandman. Every branch in me that beareth not fruit he taketh away; and every branch that beareth fruit he purgeth it, that it may bring forth more fruit. Now ye are clean through the word which I have spoken unto you. Abide in me, and I in you. As the branch cannot bear fruit of itself, except it abide in the vine; no more can ye, except ye abide in me. I am the vine, ye are the branches: He that abideth in me, and I in him, the same bringeth forth much fruit: for without me ye can do nothing. If a man abide not in me, he is cast forth as a branch, and is withered; and men gather them, and cast them into the fire, and they are burned. If ye abide in me, and my words abide in you, ye shall ask what ye will, and it shall be done unto you. Herein is my Father glorified that ye bear much fruit; so shall ye be my disciples."
> JOHN 15:1-8

Jesus laid out how and why this purging must take place. He tells us that He is the vine; we are the branches and the Father is the Husbandman. Every branch in Jesus that bears not fruit (not growing, not fighting, having no hope of being used for Gods glory in the kingdom) He takes away. Do you see that? Jesus says the Husbandman, the Father, will take away any branch that is not allowing Him to increase as they decrease or "bearing fruit." But that's not all he says. He goes on to say that every branch that *does* bear fruit will be purged by the Husbandman.

What is He saying? He is saying what we have already learned in this study, that we must be born again of God's nature to be a branch in Christ. Then he is saying what we have been talking about here in this study since we saw that Paul recognized a struggle between the old sinful, fleshly nature and the new Christ like nature within. He is saying that if you are born again, living for God and bearing fruit- that is wonderful. But that only means that God is pleased with you, and now He wants to purge you, to put you through struggles to help you see yourself and to lead you through spiritual warfare so that you come to know Him in a greater way. He wants to purge you, peel you, burn away that flesh on the altar. Why? TO BRING FORTH MORE FRUIT!

Watch what He says next in verse 3. He says, "Now ye are clean through the Word which I have spoken unto you." Why did He find it necessary to say that? I used to think that it was only because Jesus was teaching them that the purging and cleaning that He was going to do was going to take place by the Word of God; which is absolutely true. But there is another reason He said this at this point of His teaching. It's because as we go through the purging process, He doesn't want us to forget that WE ARE CLEAN! As a loving Father, he knows that when the pain, the embarrassment and the confusion of warfare comes in, we can't doubt God and his salvation work. No! Never! But we must trust in God that after being born again, there is a purging of the old man that will take place if we are ever going to produce real fruit for God's Kingdom.

In the trials and struggles of the Christian life, I've seen many people who got discouraged and turned back to the world, the flesh and the devil. But it was in those struggles that God wanted to prove them and help them. That is why in the very next verse (vs. 4) He tells us to abide in Him and let Him abide is us. Why? Again, because as a loving Father he knows that when the purging comes, that if we get outside of Him and His will, or if we don't allow Him to abide in us – then we will never last through the purging. <u>If that happens; then the trial that was supposed to strengthen us in God, and like Paul in Romans 7, bring us to a place of distrust of ourselves and total reliance on God; will instead, cause us to backslide away from God</u>. That is why in verse 5, Jesus says again, "I am the vine, ye are the branches: he that abideth in me and I in him, the same BRINGETH FORTH MUCH FRUIT." Why can He say this so assuredly? Because if we abide in Him and He abides in us, WE WILL BRING FORTH MUCH FRUIT because that is His will. That is His purpose in dealing with us. That is the reason He saves us and fills us with His Spirit. TO BRING FORTH MUCH FRUIT. The only thing that will keep that from happening is if we get outside of Him or we allow Him to depart from us because of our stubbornness and disobedience.

Lastly in verse 5 He reminds us that without Him we can do nothing. That realization only comes about in the trials. After many purgings and much warfare, Paul could declare, not out of false humility- but out of a thing learned well on the battlefield, "that in me, that is my flesh, dwelleth no good thing." Having learned from the struggles, He tells Timothy to "not be ashamed of his testimony of Paul being a prisoner." (2 Tim 1:8) "No," he assures him, "don't be ashamed of the things that I have gone through because they are the very precious things that have brought me to the place I now occupy in God." In fact, He tells Timothy, his beloved son in the Gospel, to "be thou a partaker of the afflictions of the gospel according to the power of God." Why would Paul tell his spiritual son to go and be a partaker of the kinds of awful sufferings that he himself had gone through? Because he loved him and he wanted him to experience God's best! And Paul knew better than anyone that entering into the battle and fighting the good fight was the only way to bring forth much fruit in Christ! That's why he tells Timothy to endure hardness as a good soldier and don't entangle himself with he affairs of this life. He desires him to look to be a faithful soldier, endure the trials, endure the pain; endure it all that he may please Him who has chosen him to be a soldier. It will be worth it all!

Peter picked up this very thought:

> "Beloved, think it not strange concerning the fiery trial which is to try you as though some strange thing has happened unto you: But rejoice, inasmuch as ye are partakers of Christ's sufferings: that, when his glory shall be revealed, ye may be glad also with exceeding joy. If ye be reproached for the name of Christ, happy are ye, for the spirit of Glory and of God resteth upon you: on their part he is evil spoken of, but on your part he is glorified. But let none of you suffer as a murderer, or as a thief, or as an evil-

doer, or as a busybody in other men's matters. Yet if any man suffer as a Christian, let him not be ashamed; but let him glorify God on this behalf. For the time is come, that judgment must begin at the house of God: and if it first begin at us, what shall the end be of them that obey not the gospel of God? And if the righteous scarcely be saved, where shall the ungodly and the sinner appear? Wherefore let them that suffer according to the will of God commit the keeping of their souls unto him in well doing, as unto a faithful creator."

1 Pt 4:12 -19

These things are not to seem strange to us as we go through trials and temptations. We should mature enough in God to know that this is God's dealing with His children. God deals with us so that He may receive glory from our lives. God deals with us as a loving Father, who wants the best for His children. This must remain foremost in our hearts and minds as we live through the struggles of life. This principle must govern all else, when we find ourselves in the battle to live faithful to God. It is keeping this foremost in our hearts and minds, as we desire to please Him that will cause us to bring joy to the heart of our heavenly Father.

Most of what we do today in the name of Jesus would be done away with if we put the right emphasis and teaching on the new birth. That old nature, which every man is born with after the fall, has been rejected by God and having the divine nature of God born within our hearts is our only hope of escaping the wages of death. We must be born of that incorruptible Seed, the Word of God. The seed producing after his kind, the new creation being born in the image of God, then the purging of the old nature by the trials we face. <u>These principles all work together, to strengthen the spirit man, to crucify the old nature and to sanctify the believer. Each of us must allow this process to grow us up in the things of God so that each joint can supply its part, and so that we all can grow together as lively stones into a house in which God can dwell- His church.</u>

CHAPTER SIX

The Individual and the Assembly

That Which Applies to the Individual, Must Also be Applied to the Assembly

God is now and always has been looking for a Ministry through which He can show forth His glory. God will pour out His Spirit and bring about a renewing of His Church, but He must have a vessel (or Ministry) of recovery through which to pour out that revival. That Ministry will recover or revive the true teaching of God's Holy Word, and will bring people back to the understanding of the kinds of truths that we have been learning in this study.

Everything we have said to this point in our study about the individual, we now must see how it applies to a body, the general assembly or any ministry. As a Ministry, the same principles of <u>God's rejection of the old/fallen nature</u>, the <u>need for the Seed to birth a new life,</u> as well as <u>the struggle of the old nature versus the new nature</u>, each applies to a local assembly just as they do to the individual. The principles <u>of sanctification of the new creation</u>, the <u>purging of the old man/old ways</u>, and <u>the purpose of the trials in our life</u> also apply to a ministry as much as they do in the life of an individual.

A Ministry Born of God

If any ministry will be used of God for revival, it will have to be a ministry that is born of God. True revival has never come, and never will come, through a ministry that was not born of God's calling. Jeremiah speaks of preachers that went out to preach but God says "I sent them not." That kind of ministry can never be used of God for revival. Any ministry of revival will have come to understand that God has totally rejected the old fallen nature of man. Thus, such a ministry will understand that God will never use anything of the old carnal, fleshly man. Therefore, that ministry will have had to reject anything that comes out of the natural mind, will have nothing to do with man's programs of religion, and will not rely on anything but the leadership of the Holy Ghost.

Such a ministry will know that anything that they do for God, must come out of that which is born of God, and not from anything that man has his corrupted hands in. Any direction or any work that such a ministry undertakes must come from that which is born from God.

Anything done must come out of the receiving of the Word to birth a new life. Every outreach, every service, every motive must be something that is born of an incorruptible Word that will bring forth after its kind. <u>Only that which comes to a ministry from God, can produce the life of God in a ministry.</u> Any program of man, any growth program, any flesh pleasing program, any program that uses the entertainments of the world to draw the world is not born from God; and it will bring forth after its kind; and that kind is carnal. And that which is carnal can only bring forth death.

Any time in history where God truly poured out His Spirit and where there has been true revival; it never has come except it was birthed by God in the heart of a man of God or in the hearts of a faithful remnant. Revival only comes from that which is ordained by God, not by man.

{I know I'm being a little redundant here. But we have to see the parallels between all that we have studied about the individual and how these things must also take place and be present in any ministry that God will use to bring about revival and recover what has been lost in our present day church teaching.}

Any ministry that will be used of God will have gone through the process of "sanctification of the new man." A ministry must go through the process of being sanctified unto God, just like an individual. The sanctification will take place as that ministry goes through the struggle of building up the new man and putting down the old nature – just like the individual. The "purging of the old man/old ways," must take place for the ministry of God just like it does in the individual. Any ministry that God can use to bring about a revival will have undergone the purging of God that it may bring forth more fruit unto the husbandman.

Of course, such a ministry will have come to understand the purpose of its trials in order for it to grow. Its growth through such trials is what God will use to make that ministry strong and full of conviction, so that God can use it for His glory. <u>History is filled with stories of ministries that didn't understand the struggles, and God never did get any glory from such ministries. Man may have gotten glory,</u>

people may have been made to feel good, beautiful build-ings may have been built; **but all was for naught because God was not given glory.**

We are living in the last days, and Jesus is going to take His true Church home very soon. God will show forth His glory one more time-through His elect bride remnant so that the world will know, one last time, who God is and what His church should have been all along!

That vessel/ministry of revival will be marked by one overwhelming thing- THE LIFE OF JESUS CHRIST. That Church that He is coming for will be nothing less than what it was when it was born on the day of Pentecost. Jesus said that the gates of hell will not prevail against His Church. If Jesus comes back and receives for himself a Church that is less than what He started with, then the gates of hell will have prevailed, and Jesus will have failed. Impossible!

What did He start with? He started with a Church alive with the very Spirit of Jesus. In the book of Acts, we see God talking to, directing and empowering a people accord-ing to His will.

In chapter two the Holy Ghost fills the Church with the promise of the Father and they speak with other tongues about the greatness of God. In chapter two Peter preaches and three thousand ask what they must do to be saved by Jesus. In the third chapter, Peter and John heal a man in the name of Jesus. In the fourth, the Apostles are jailed and the council takes note that they had been with Jesus. They are threatened not to preach the name of Jesus; but the apostles would rather obey Jesus than man. The Church has a prayer meeting to thank God for the persecution and the building shakes, and they are filled again with the Holy Spirit. In the fifth chapter, sin tries to enter in through two hypocrites lying to the Holy Ghost and God kills them, and the fear of Jesus comes on all the people.

Signs and wonders are performed in the name of Jesus, Peter's shadow heals those laying by the road side, they are re-arrested and an angel lets Peter out of jail. Stephen does signs and wonders, preaches a message that covers from Abraham to Christ and as they stone him he sees Jesus in heaven. In the eighth chapter, God grants Phillip miracles in Samaria, the Apostles come to help him preach and the Holy Spirit falls on the people. Phillip then preaches to and baptizes a government official and is then carried down the road by the hand of God to continue preaching. In the next chapter, Saul is knocked off his horse by Jesus, and is baptized by a man who was specifically told to go and do it. Then God speaks in perfect detail to Cornelius, and tells him where to go to find a man that will instruct his house in the things of God. Peter is told they are coming and to go and preach. Now the gentiles are getting saved and filled, because Jesus is being preached. This exactness and power of God's leadership continues on chapter after chapter in the Book of Acts.

Does this sound like our Church today? No? This is, however, what He is coming back for. And this is what His vessel of revival will be, <u>but that vessel will do what He commands</u>. The vessel (ministry) of revival will have rejected the old nature just as God has rejected it. That ministry will not try to repackage anything of the flesh and the old nature and force it upon God. A ministry of revival will seek only those things that are born after the Seed/Word of God that will bring forth after His kind. The programs of the flesh and religion will have no place in such a ministry because it will only seek that which comes from God. That ministry will have come to maturity by the struggles and battles that God will have brought it through. And through those trials that ministry will have become patient, perfect and entire, wanting nothing. It certainly won't want the wealth and fame of this world. It will be a vessel for revival. It will be a Church that hell cannot prevail against. It will be a vessel, like the candlestick in Revelations, all of gold within and without; it will be a vessel filled with Jesus!

A Ministry That Will Trust Only in God

In 2 Kings Chapter 2, we see a picture of the ministry when God tells the prophet to get a new cruse. There is a problem, and God tells the prophet to use a new bowl to put salt into the water to heal the poison in the water. Of course, God could have told the prophet to throw the salt directly into the water, but He instructs the man of God to get a new cruse in order to have a vessel through which to pour out the healing, the salt. There must be a vessel through which God can pour out the healing and deliverance of Himself.

Notice that it was to be a *new* cruse. It was to a new vessel created by God for the task of pouring out the healing. God can never use an old, stale, dry ministry for revival.

Jesus said <u>we are the salt </u>of the earth. We (the Jesus in us) are to be poured out as the answer, the healing and the blessing of God. As we have already seen, we are not really the blessing. No, we are nothing. But the nature, power and love of God in us is to make us the <u>Salt of the earth</u>.

<u>The Church has made the awful mistake in thinking that she is the blessing.</u> We have forgotten that what we are is a rejected thing, an unholy thing. However, if we are born of God's seed and will bring forth after His kind, and will contain God; then we are a vessel of God. We are still nothing of ourselves, but if we contain God, and will obey Him, then He will command us. And if we do as He commands, then nothing shall be impossible to His Church. God is still looking for a new vessel through which to pour out His Spirit. The Church is going to have to come to the place where all else dies (just like we have already looked at in the life of the individual); and there is a rebirth by God's spirit. Anything short of this, will be forcing that old flesh on God. Any ministry that God can really use must be a NEW VESSEL. A vessel that knows that unless God comes and breathes life into it, there is no hope. A vessel of revival must have seen that there is an un-crossable chasm between God and man, and that only by God given life can there be a nature born into a Church that will make it a vessel of God. Such a ministry will need to have rejected all of the old man, and will have to come to a place where it understands that whatever struggles and trials it faces, it is for the purpose of God working out His glory in that Church. Thus we see, what is true for the individual is true for the Church as a whole.

A Beginning and An End

"And the child Samuel ministered unto the Lord before Eli. And the word of the Lord was precious in those days; there was no open vision. And it came to pass at that time, when Eli was laid down in his place, and his eyes began to wax dim, that he would not see; And ere the lamp of God went out in the temple of the Lord, where the ark of God was, and Samuel was laid down to sleep; That the Lord called Samuel: and he answered, Here am I. And he ran unto Eli and said, Here am I; for thou calledst me. And he said, I called not; lie down again. And he went and lay down. And the Lord called yet again, Samuel. And Samuel arose and went to Eli, and said, Here am I; for thou didst call me. And he answered, I called not, my son; lie down again. Now Samuel did not yet know the Lord, neither was the word of the Lord yet revealed unto him. And the Lord called Samuel again the third time. And he arose and went to Eli, and said, Here am I; for thou didst call me. And Eli perceived that the Lord had called the child. Therefore Eli said unto Samuel, Go, lie down: and it shall be, if he call thee, that thou shalt say, Speak, Lord; for thy servant heareth. So Samuel went and laid down in his place. And the Lord came, and stood, and called as at other times, Samuel, Samuel. Then Samuel answered, Speak; for thy servant heareth. And the Lord said to Samuel, Behold, I will do a thing in Israel, at which both the ears of everyone that heareth it shall tingle. In that day I will perform against Eli all things which I have spoken concerning his house: when I begin I will also make

an end. For I have told him that I will judge
his house forever for the iniquity which he
knoweth; because his sons made themselves
vile, and he restrained them not."
                    1 SAMUEL 3:1-13

God calls a new vessel, Samuel, to be His chosen Ministry. God is going to raise up a ministry that will operate as
God wants it to. But look at how God called that ministry.
As He calls this new ministry of Samuel (the new ministry
after God's own heart) God does something very important.

When God called Samuel, the first thing He spoke to
him was *not* how great Samuel was going to be for God.
No! The first thing God let Samuel know was that He was
going to judge the ministry of Eli, because of it's iniquity
before God. Why would God call a young boy, and the first
thing He speaks to Him about is the judgment of Eli's ministry? Remember, Samuel doesn't even know the voice of
God yet; that's why He went to Eli three times when God
first tried to speak to Him. So why would God speak such
things, that will make every ear tingle when heard, about a
judgment upon Eli's ministry to a young boy that is just
starting out in ministry?

Are you seeing it yet? God spoke to Samuel (who represents the new ministry, the new cruse, the new vessel of
revival, the young boy, the new creature) and He told him
right up front that I WILL NOT USE A VESSEL OF THE
OLD SINFULL NATURE. I WILL NOT SHARE MY GLORY
WITH THE FLESH. And any ministry, <u>ANY MINSTRY</u>-
(no matter who it is, what name it has on it or even if I
originally called it and anointed it) THAT DISPLEASES ME;
I WILL JUDGE IT AND REJECT IT FROM BEFORE ME!

God was making that new ministry know assuredly that He is God and without Him we have no hope of heaven. In other words, there was a total rejection of the old sinful nature and that if Samuel was going to have any future with God; he would have to know that God hates the old sinful man. This is a type of God's dealing with anyone that will come to Him for salvation or any ministry that will desire to be a ministry of revival.

In verse twelve, God tells Samuel, that He will make a beginning (the birth of a new creature/ministry/vessel) and an end at the same time (the rejection of the old sinful nature that God hates). <u>That's always the way it is.</u>

Anytime there is going to be a ministry that God will use to bring a revival, there will come also an end of all that is old. By "old" we simply mean anything that is not born of God. We mean anything that has grown stale because it was received second hand. Anything that has not been made real in the proving fires of God will be left by such a ministry. Religious traditions must be rejected by the new ministry because God will not use what man has defiled. The ministry that God will raise up for revival will be a new beginning, born only of the Spirit of God by that seed which will bring forth after His own kind. <u>God was making it very clear to Samuel that "if you want to obey me, then I will make you a beginning, a vessel of revival, a ministry that represents God." But God was also letting Samuel know right from the very beginning, that "if you (Samuel) ever decide that you don't need God or that somehow you are something good by yourself, then I will reject you just like I am doing with Eli."</u>

God will not deal with that flesh! God has rejected that kind of being. God will, in his mercy, purge and cleanse that old nature from his vessel of revival. He will do this in any ministry that He will use, just like he does it in an individual.

In these last days, if God is going to have a ministry that He can use to bring about an end time revival, a Church that is truly filled with Jesus like He started with; then that ministry will have come to know that it will be born of God, that the old sinful godless nature of man can have no part in governing that ministry. It will have to be a ministry through which God can flow. It will be a ministry born of God, not evolved out of the religious confusion of today's Babylon system. There will be no evolving of the fleshly, self glorifying, man centered, man educated, lust filled ministries. No, such kinds will not evolve into something God will use. God's vessels will not have evolved from the witchcraft we call "power" in the church today. God's ministry will be born of God's Spirit as it comes to see itself as without hope before a Holy God and cries out to God in repentance.

History Shows the Beginning Comes Out Of An End

Do we see the rejection of all old things in ministries that God has used in the past? Samuel himself was a new beginning, even in the fact of his conception. It was only the hand of God opening his mother's womb that allowed Samuel to even be born. God told Jeremiah that He knew him before he was even born- a new beginning; he was not called of man but of God. Daniel has nothing to evolve from; he was a captive in a heathen land, and all about him

were doing whatever they could do just to survive in captivity. But Daniel 1:8 says that Daniel "purposed in his heart
not to defile himself." Daniel was a new beginning in the
midst of a people's total rejection of God, and in the midst
of God's judgment for such rejection. Joseph was taken
from his family, put in a dungeon, just so God could empty
all hope of mankind out of him. He was separated from all
he knew, all he trusted and all he loved. Then God could
have a new vessel to use mightily and to bring about the
saving of God's people.

Jesus started by gathering 12 men. They were ignorant; they were hated tax collectors and lowly fishermen
that couldn't evolve into anything. If that wasn't enough,
he further purged them, broke them, and chastised them
with their unbelief. They gave up jobs and family to follow
Him, and still he looked at them and said, "Will you go
also?" Once, He told them that they didn't even know what
Spirit they were of. Then, when they were emptied out
and thought they couldn't be more broken; one of their
own betrayed Him. They watched as He was tortured, He
was hung on a cursed tree, died in front of them and was
put into a grave. Then when they were hiding in a room,
totally without hope, Jesus came. The Lord opened to them
all things in the scriptures concerning himself, filled them
with the Holy Ghost and established them as His ministry.

Wigglesworth was an illiterate plumber. Evan Roberts
was a skinny teenager. Bro. Seymour had no illustrious
clerical background and seemed any unlikely vessel through
which to pour out the Azusa Street revival. But when he
was praying 7 hours a day, he asked God, why there was no
real revival and God told him, "Because you don't pray

enough." (Recently, in my own studies, God has allowed me to learn of many, many men and ministries that produced great miracles and preached the truth; and they saw revivals that sound like they came right out of the pages of the Book of Acts.) They were all men or ministries that had prayed through to a fresh vision of God!

Who were the men that really shook the kingdom of darkness and stormed the beaches of sin to establish the Kingdom of God? There have been countless moves of God throughout history that show us, that God is looking for the vessel in which there is no hope (human hope). The greatest preachers, the greatest revivals and the greatest ministries have always come through vessels that have turned from the old sinful flesh entirely. Ministries that through the struggles and trials of the Christian walk, had come to be God's vessels through which he could poor out Himself!

Bro. Bartlemen, in his book on the Azusa Street revival, ends with one of the most profound things I've ever read outside of the scriptures, and I've never forgotten it. Years after the Azusa Street fires had begun to die down; he was deep in prayer one night asking God to see the move of God again. God told him, "If you could only become small enough I could use you." Oh God, let us become small enough!!

God has no problem pouring out a revival- He just needs a vessel that will be born of Him, and after being born of Him, that ministry will have to be purged by its trials and grow into what God wants it to be.

A Ministry Will Be Purged

In Judges Chapter 7, we see how God will deal with a ministry. Gideon has 32,000 in his church. God tells him that he has too many. Why? God will not allow the old man to glory in His presence. God tells Gideon, "You have too many here for me to give you the victory. If I give you the victory with this mega church membership you will think that you did it by the flesh." God began to whittle down Gideon's membership. God sends home everyone that is afraid; and 22,000 leave. It is still too many because He knows how deceitful that sinful heart is, and God knows that they will still glory in the flesh if He gives them the victory. Then God tells Gideon to have the rest of the membership come to a restful place, and take note of the faithful who keep their guard up and are faithful to the end. All but 300 show themselves to be careless. Now the ministry is down to 300 chosen vessels. Why?

Because any church that God will really use, the people will know it was God, and God will see to it that He receives all the glory. Every ministry that has really affected it's generation for God went through the purging and the testing.

There have been many military battles throughout history. Do we ever talk about the great victory where 50,000 men beat an army of 9,000 men? Does the History channel ever produce long documentaries on wars where the victor won easily because everything favored them? Of course not, there is nothing impressive about that!

A ministry that God wants to use to pour out a true revival will be a ministry that will be different than the mega foolishness we call church today. A ministry of revival will have to go through being laughed at by those of the religious sects. A ministry of revival will have people point at it and call it a cult. A ministry of revival will have others saying "you don't have to do all that to go to heaven." A ministry of revival will go through the purging and pruning of the husbandman in order to have it bring forth more fruit.

Have you ever seen a rose bush or a fruit tree that has been thoroughly pruned so that it will bring forth more blooms or more fruit the next season? I can tell you that they don't look pretty when they are pruned. The most abundantly fruitful apple trees don't even look like trees. They are cut back so far they almost look like ugly shrubs. A rose bush that produces large, gorgeous blooms looks just about dead the previous fall when it is pruned back.

So it is with God's true church. Others will look at it and mock. The religious, the old rejected nature of man, will joke because the vessel God is dealing with doesn't have 500 people in Sunday school – it has a dozen in all night prayer. The religious will think it strange that a ministry of revival doesn't have a choir of 300, but it has a few who sing unto the Lord in spirit and in truth; who fast over their worship that it would be anointed of God.

Whatever it looks like, whatever it feels like, a ministry that God will use to bring about revival must go through the battles and trials in order that it will know the faithfulness of God. Such a ministry will go through very difficult times as God eliminates those that are there for the loaves and the fishes; but not really committed to God. Such purgings will bring about a death to the self life in that ministry. And the purging will show that ministry of revival where it really is in God, not where it thinks it is!

It Is God That Grows His Church

> "Ye also, as lively stones, are built up a spiritual house, an holy priesthood, to offer up spiritual sacrifices, acceptable to God by Jesus Christ. Wherefore also it is contained in *the scripture, Behold, I lay in Zion a chief cornerstone, elect, precious: and he that believeth on him shall not be confounded.*"
>
> 1 Pt. 2:5&6

> "And are built upon the foundation of the apostles and prophets, Jesus Christ himself being the chief cornerstone; In whom all the building fitly framed together groweth unto an holy temple in the Lord: In whom ye also are builded together for an habitation of God through the Spirit."
>
> Ephesians 2:20-22.

God speaks about building a spiritual house, a vessel of revival. We are the lively stones of that house that He is building. Jesus himself is the cornerstone of that house.

We see that the entire ministry is built on the foundation of the apostles and prophets with Jesus Christ the chief cornerstone. And in Jesus the entire ministry fits together perfectly because it is born all of one blood – the blood of Jesus. Remember, it is born into the kingdom, and cannot grow into the kingdom. And after it is framed by the blood of Jesus (in the new birth after the Word of God,) it *then grows* unto a holy temple of the Lord. And we, each person or part, are being built (by the struggles God allows) together for a habitation of God through His spirit (not through the spirit of religion or of evil mankind). We must know that the foundation of God stands sure (2 Tm. 2:19), no matter what we see or feel.

These scriptures show us plainly, that for any ministry to be used of God, that vessel will have to know that it is God who will grow it. God is the foundation and God grows it, not man. Do you now see the error of "church growth programs?" God will grow His church by His Spirit! It is His work, it is His church. Those who are busy pointing out what others are doing wrong, but have no grace of God to show a better way, will be sent home by the spirit of God – just as he sent home the 31,700 of Gideon's church. Those who join such a ministry for the music, for the pastor, for the friends, for the loaves and the fishes will find it tiring after a while and will leave. They will have been purged and not even know it.

Those who come for any other reason than Jesus, and to know Him and to make Him known to others will, in the end, leave or will be purged by the trials that God sends. This vessel will not grow by the games and programs of religious denominations.

Look at the growth God desires. Look at how God grows His church through the trials of life, through the proving of His children. Why does He grow His church this way? Because God has a purpose for this growth, to get glory for Himself! He will not share His glory with another and He will grow His church.

Man has learned that there are ways in which to force things to grow. A farmer can force a cow to grow faster than it normally would. However, he only forces growth on the stock that he intends to butcher. The stock he wants to keep and breed in order to have the best herd is not forced to grow. The same is true for a pig; you fatten the ones you want to butcher not the ones you want to breed. That vessel that God will use for revival will not be forced to grow with church growth programs.

It is the Devil that will add error to a church, then he will promote it until it is big, until it is a mega error, then the devil can use it to promote his false doctrine of the humanistic gospel. He promotes it, forces it to grow, and makes it big: to slaughter it!

Athletes have learned that with steroids and growth hormones you can force the physical body to grow. In the beginning, muscle mass is packed on at a fantastic rate. People get excited because of the growth. It looks good. The body looks strong. But after a while the body will begin to break down. The super strong that have lived with these fantastic physiques; who could run faster, last longer, lift more than others around them and looked the picture of health, where do they end up? I could fill the next ten pages with the horrible side effects of forcing this type of growth on the human body. I don't need to tell of the strongest of men who die of cancers and tumors of all types: and at very young ages. Why does it happen? Because when we force growth in the human body, it will eventually destroy itself.

The scriptures warn us of the danger of adding to the body that which is of the world, of allowing the doctrines of devils to have their place among the body. When we force the growth of a ministry by adding to it that which is not born of God, we set it up for destruction like the ministry of Eli. It may look good to some for a while. It may seem to some to be exciting, or that the ministry is growing. However all that is being done is that we are adding tares, where God wanted wheat. And eventually that body will consume itself. The scripture says that such kind will bite and devour one another (Gal 5:19). Don't we see the list of ministries that played the games of religion, looked good to many, but in the end, sin and the flesh destroyed them?

Only God Can Add To A Ministry

> "Praising God, and having favour with all the people. And the Lord added to the church daily, such as should be saved."
>
> ACT 2:47

We read here that <u>the Lord added to the Church such as should be saved.</u> God added. How does God add? He brings the person to a vision of themselves, where they see their sin and know that God has rejected them. They can then cry out to God for forgiveness, knowing that they have no other hope. God hears the cry of repentance and comes in mercy and grace and washes clean in the blood of Jesus. That is how God adds to His church. When we think we can add to the church, we are in big trouble with God. We can't add anything or anybody to the church. If *we* are doing it, then all we're doing is trying to grow a sinner into a saint and that (as we have already seen) doesn't work. God adds such as should be saved. "Such as should be saved," means that they have been convicted and have <u>come to God in the right way of repentance</u>.

Did it ever occur to us that if there are those who "should be saved" then there are those who "shouldn't be saved?" (Now don't close the book now and say that I believe that some are predetermined to go to hell. That is not what the Scripture teaches, and that is not what we are saying here. The Bible says that Jesus died for the whole world and as many as will hear the call of our God and believe will be saved. John 3, Romans 10 and many other scriptures show that God's will is that none would perish.) But some "should not be saved" simply refers to those who have not allowed God to deal with them concerning their sin, the old man and their need for salvation. In these souls, there will be no real cry of repentance, no change of nature, and no planting of that incorruptible seed that can bring forth after its kind. These, are they that get added to a church by man not by God. And these are they that God calls tares, not wheat. And it is these that we have now filled our churches with, and we have brought a shame to the name of God and to his house!

If the scriptural standard is kept in place, then only God can add to His church. If that standard is lowered, then all kinds of things will end up in that church- but then it isn't God's Church any more. If you lower the standard, you can attract a big crowd. Men who do such are not pastors of sheep, they are herders of goats. Congregations are filled with goats that buck and fight at every thing, not sheep that are controlled with the spoken word of their master. Such places will not be vessels for revival unless God is allowed to purge them of the flesh.

God's true servants know that there job is to keep the Church pure so that it can be a clean vessel that God can flow through. All else is secondary to this effort. If we draw people to a ministry with _anything other than Jesus,_ then we will have to keep them entertained _with everything but Jesus._ Israel complained that all they had was "this manna to eat." They wanted something else, something that satisfied their flesh. Later, Jesus came and declared that "I am the bread that came down from heaven." When they complained that they wanted something else, they were actually saying we want something other than Jesus, something that tickles the flesh. A ministry of revival will seek nothing but God, and will look for the growth that only comes through God's dealing with souls. God will add to His church such as He sees should be saved! People do not join such a church. No right hand of fellowship will bring a soul into this kind of church. No amount of money can be given and no paper work can be filed that will make someone a member of this kind of church. This is God's Church we are talking about now. No, a soul must be born of the Spirit of God into this kind of church.

God's plan is set. It has been set from before the foundation of the world. In these last days God will have a Holy remnant, a peculiar people, a bride, a Church. That Church will reject what He has rejected and will love what He loves. That bride will be made up of those who belong to Him. It will be made up of those who will have come to God in repentance and will allow God to purge them as He sees fit and that remnant will give glory to Jesus. That bride will have made herself ready for her Lord!

God will have a vessel of revival.

God will pour out of His mighty Spirit upon His Church

God will, one last time, have a true Church that will show forth His Glory.

God will have a Church that will shake the kingdom of darkness one more time.

God will return to earth for a Church that represents His thought and His truth.

God will take a Church home with him before He destroys this sin sick world.

God will have a remnant Church for a bride; the only question is whether or not you and I will be a part of it.

To contact the Author, please write to:
Bro. Richard Goebel
"A Sower Went Forth to Sow"
PO BOX 121
CHELTENHAM, PA 19012

To order additional copies of

The Lie of Spiritual Evolution

have your credit card ready and call
1 800-917-BOOK (2665)

or e-mail
orders@selahbooks.com

or order online at
www.selahbooks.com